T0207725

Love Lifted Me

A devotional

KELLY FERGUSON

WESTBOW
PRESS®
A DIVISION OF THOMAS NELSON
& ZONDERVAN

WestBow Press books may be ordered through booksellers or by contacting:

WestBow Press
A Division of Thomas Nelson & Zondervan
1663 Liberty Drive
Bloomington, IN 47403
www.westbowpress.com
1 (866) 928-1240

ISBN: 978-1-9736-7361-3 (sc)
ISBN: 978-1-9736-7360-6 (e)

Print information available on the last page.

WestBow Press rev. date: 10/17/2019

Dedication

I dedicate this book to all those who encouraged me to write, supported me in this effort, helped with editing, and patiently waited for me to complete this book. I am especially grateful to my family, my Ohio and Tennessee church families, my therapists, my co-workers, my Word Weavers Knoxville Chapter, and my many other friends.

Sadly, a few of my biggest supporters passed away before I was finished. I dedicate this book in remembrance of them: Floss Waggoner, Mary McKinney, Carroll Southards, Lorraine Smith, and Lillian Tanner. God used these special people to coax this work out of me and to encourage me along the journey.

A special thank you to my mom and biggest fan, Karen Wilson; my best friend and editor, Marty Teffeteller; my long-time cheerleaders, the Forest Hill Baptist Church Ruth Class, Karen Robinson, Lillian Mayes, and Judy Rice; and those who pushed me across the finish line, Judy Rainwater, Megan Marcus, and Debra Jenkins. I am incredibly blessed to have you in my life.

Preface

This book is truly a journey from fear to faith, from defeat to victory, and from pain to passion. It is a book I didn't set out to write. It wasn't in my plans or even on my radar. Who am I to write a book? What do I have to say that others would find interesting or intriguing? With what authority do I speak? I wondered if anyone would even read it. Despite these doubts and fears, with this book, I have finally become a published author.

This book is born of God. It is His loving pursuit of my heart, which was once an angry, severely damaged heart housed in the soul of a broken woman. I was mired in overwhelming emotional pain from past abuse and the death of my husband from cancer at the young age of thirty-three. I felt like God's victim, and I didn't think He cared about me. I needed help.

Somehow, I found my way to therapy, and through therapy, I discovered journaling. My journal was my safe place. I could yell at God and pour out my soul on the pages, and the pages wouldn't judge me. My agonizing pain and sadness filled several volumes of journals, and with each finished page, I found myself one step closer to healing.

Then one day I reached a life-changing realization: God didn't inflict my trauma. Rather, I was a casualty of the broken and diseased world in which we live, a fallen world inhabited by free-willed people who make horrible decisions that hurt innocent people. I could clearly see evidence in my writing of how God was with me in the bad times. He was the reason I survived it. He actually did love me, and my being convinced of this love changed everything. It was the beginning of a new, closer walk with God.

God then set about working all this out for my good. He took my writing to the next level by providing an opportunity to write on a daily basis. I was asked by the church where I work to write daily devotions for the church's online prayer list. Next thing I knew, people were talking about my devotions and the distribution list was growing longer. Over a hundred people received them daily, and these readers were forwarding them to countless friends and relatives. These faithful readers then encouraged me to write this book, and they have waited a long time to finally hold it in their hands and share it with others.

This is an unfolding story and an ongoing conversation. It is God revealing Himself to me through scripture in my everyday life and in ordinary situations. There is no order to this work; it is just God as He works out His plan and purpose for my life.

I am glad you are taking this journey with me. It is an honor to walk beside you. I pray that you will be inspired and encouraged as you read this book and that your relationship with God will grow deeper as He speaks to you. Most of all though, I hope and pray that you will finish the book wholeheartedly believing that God loves and adores you deeply. This message changed my life, and I hope it changes yours.

Bible Translation Abbreviations

AMP – Amplified Bible
BSB – Berean Study Bible
CSB – Christian Standard Bible
CEV – Contemporary English Version
ERV – Easy-to-Read Version
ESV – English Standard Version
GW – GOD'S WORD Translation
KJV – King James Version
TLB – Living Bible
MSG – The Message
NASB – New American Standard Bible
NCV – New Century Version
NIV – New International Version
NKJV– New King James Version
NLT – New Living Translation
TPT – The Passion Translation
Berean Study Bible retrieved from biblehub.com.
All other versions are retrieved from biblegateway.com.

Do It for Me

❤

"Trust God from the bottom of your heart; don't try to
figure out everything on your own" (Proverbs 3:5 MSG).

I have written devotions for years, devotions which have taken on a
life of their own. Many readers of these have encouraged me to write
a book. I struggled with my confidence and felt that writing a book was
too daunting a task for me. Turns out I was right: it was not within my
power to do so nor was it the proper time.

I struggled for years with indecision until God suddenly began to
move the process along. First, I received a call one day from a self-
publishing company I had contacted years previously, asking me to
seriously reconsider publication. Still hesitant, I sought counsel from a
dear friend. She gave me the same encouragement others had given me,
yet this time, my heart finally heard. She helped me to see how God can
inspire others through my stories and my thoughts. I could share God's
love with my readers which I felt passionate about doing.

The next morning, the Saturday before Easter, I woke up surprised
to hear God speaking to me. I distinctly heard Him say, "Just do it for
Me; please do it for Me." Peace suddenly washed over me. I knew God
was giving me motivation and His blessing. I knew He would walk this
unknown path with me, and He wanted to use my efforts for His glory.

That same morning, the publisher's representative called me. He
explained that he didn't usually work on Saturdays, but he felt God's
direction to call me. He was very kind and calming; he addressed each
of my fears with understanding and patience. It was clear that God was
moving and had brought me to this defining moment. It was definitely
the time to pursue my dream.

Although I still struggle, knowing that I have God's clear blessing
has made me excited for the future. I can't wait to see what He is going to

do with my little offering. I pray that He uses it to inspire and encourage everyone who reads it.

Sometimes God calls us to do a task that we feel is beyond our capabilities. As we count the costs and weigh the difficulties, we need to remember that God does not call us to do something that He won't help us complete. He is the difference between what we think we can do and what we actually accomplish. We will feel God's power in a whole new way as we achieve more than we ever thought possible, and we will glorify God in the process.

> "[May God] equip you with everything good that you may do his will, working in us that which is pleasing in his sight, through Jesus Christ, to whom be glory forever and ever. Amen" (Hebrews 13:21 ESV).

Here Comes the Bride, But Where Is Her Groom?

> "Let us rejoice and be glad and give him glory! For the wedding of the Lamb has come and His bride has made herself ready" (Revelation 19:7 NIV).

On September 4, 1987, my fiancé and I eloped to Cumberland Falls State Park in Kentucky, two years from the day that we started dating. We were two impulsive college kids who were tired of spending our summers living three states apart. The fact that we had no real means of support was not even a concern; we were too in love to care about that minor point.

We were proud to be the talk of the campus that day. Our college student services personnel heard of our plans and tried their best to talk us out of it, but we didn't listen. We were determined. Our friends pitched in and helped us, one friend lending me a dress and helping me with my hair and makeup, another pastor friend volunteering to perform the ceremony. Others attended the wedding and threw us a surprise wedding reception.

Per the tradition, we did not see or talk to each other that day. I was to concentrate on getting ready, and he was in charge of finding a location at the Falls. Since we didn't communicate, I discovered upon my arrival that I didn't know the exact location of the wedding, and it was getting too dark to look for the wedding party. As I anxiously stood in the parking lot, a friend suddenly appeared, locked his arm in mine, and escorted me as if he were giving me away. Then, as if in a romantic movie, I turned a corner and there stood my fiancé and the wedding party on a pier overlooking the beautiful waterfall.

When I think about this story, I am reminded of the analogy of Christ and His bride. We, the church, are collectively called His bride, and He dearly loves us. We are tasked with making preparations for His return, the day when He will take us to live with Him. We do not know exactly when that will be, so we are to be ever vigilant, dedicating ourselves to getting spiritually ready. Just as my friend sought me, we are asked to go out and find those who do not know Jesus as their personal savior so they can be ready too. If we don't, they may never find their way, and sadly they may miss this truly wonderful day.

> "Then the angel said to me, 'Write this: Blessed are those who are invited to the wedding supper of the Lamb!' And he added, 'These are the true words of God'" (Revelation 19:9 NIV).

God, My Victorious Healer

"But thanks be to God! He gives us the victory through
our Lord Jesus Christ" (2 Corinthians 2:14 NIV).

"For I am the Lord, who heals you" (Exodus 15:26b NIV).

These two verses, though quite different, go hand-in-hand. God's
healing, whether physically, emotionally, or spiritually, is a victory.
God is the victorious healer for whatever we battle.

For twenty-four months, my 31-year old husband and I fought hard
against Glioblastoma, an aggressive brain cancer, which was already at stage
four when it was discovered. We went through surgeries and traditional
treatments, researched and tried new treatments, traveled to different
doctors and out-of-state hospitals, called on churches and friends to pray,
held prayer services, and did all that we could do to make this cancer go
away. However, the victorious healing did not come in life but in death. By
the time that we had run this course, there was not much of a quality of
life left for him or for us. His body was battled and broken beyond human
repair, and the best plan for him was to pass from this life into the next.

I then began my time of grief. In time, I was able to start working
toward my healing from my husband's death and the subsequent anger
and depression. I spent hours and hours in counseling, struggling hard to
emerge from this heavy sadness. Eventually, I was able to arise from the
depression and finally release the grief. I realized that while my husband
is gone, I still carry him with me in my memories, and I still see him in
my daughter, who is very much like him. I no longer feel the heavy grief
that emotionally bound me to him every day.

It's been a long, hard journey, but looking back I can see how God
carried me through the healing process from a slow start to a victorious
finish. He graciously provided leadership and put qualified people in my
life when I needed their help and advice. Because of this loving support
and guidance, I am no longer stuck in perpetual sadness, and I can now
go forward in my life wherever He leads.

God can provide the victory from whatever keeps us bound in sin, sadness, anger, bitterness, or unforgiveness. He is our constant source of help and strength. He takes that first step with us at the beginning of our journey, holds our hand and encourages us along the way, directs each of our steps as we follow, and victoriously walks across the finish line with us as we step into a new life.

> "For the Lord your God is the one who goes with you to fight for you against your enemies to give you victory" (Deuteronomy 20:4 NIV).

The Precious Gift of Snow Boots

> "*That's* how much you mean to me! *That's* how much I love you! I'd sell off the whole world to get you back, trade the creation just for you" (Isaiah 43:4 MSG).

Seeing snow always makes me homesick and nostalgic. I grew up in Ohio where there was snow piled on the ground steadily from October to March. We always had fun on snow days, playing games inside and pelting each other with snow outside. When I grew up and became a mom, I was able to enjoy the snow once again as I played outside and drank hot chocolate with my own daughter.

There was one particular snow day I will always cherish which happened when my daughter was around five or six years old. Her dad, my late husband, worked third shift, and that particular night it snowed several inches. Before coming home, he went by a store and bought a new pair of tiny blue snow boots adorned with a much-loved dinosaur character on the sides. Then he came home and patiently waited for our daughter to wake up so she could put on her coat and new boots and go outside to play in the snow with him before he went to bed.

I still have these precious boots as keepsakes for her. I love to hold them and look at them. I hope when she holds them, they remind her of that day and she fondly remembers her dad's spontaneity, his genuine love and care for her, and his great delight in her.

This story illustrates the personal love of God. He not only knows us individually, but He loves us individually. He watches over us and gets involved in our lives. He hears our prayers and meets our needs. He gives us each gifts, talents, and passions with which we can enrich our lives and edify Him. He delights in us, celebrating our accomplishments and mourning our losses. He enjoys being with us and anticipates our visits with Him. His love and His lordship are personal to every single one of us.

> "The Lord your God is with you. He is a hero who saves you. He happily rejoices over you, renews you with his love, and celebrates over you with shouts of joy" (Zephaniah 3:17 GW).

He Will Help Us Through

> "When you pass through the waters, I will be with you; and through the rivers, they will not overflow you. When you walk through the fire, you will not be scorched, nor will the flame burn you" (Isaiah 43:2 NASB).

This verse is often a go-to verse when we are feeling overwhelmed by life and its circumstances. I have heard several messages on this verse, and often preachers and teachers point out that the verse begins with the word "when" and not with the word "if," meaning hard times are inevitable and not just a mere possibility. However, God pointed out something new to me in the passage: He does not say, "I will stop the waters or the fire"; He says, "I will go through them with you."

The word "through" has several definitions. It means moving in one side and out the other side of something or somewhere. It also means continuing in time toward completion; or to have completed a process or a collection. In reference to a phone, it means establishing a connection with someone. If we apply these definitions to this verse, we get a better picture. We have a connection with God; therefore, He walks with us from the beginning to the end of a hardship, all the way through to completion.

The biblical picture I get is of the Israelites' journey from Egypt to the Promised Land. The people had escaped Egypt, yet they faced a journey through the daunting wilderness. God led them day and night. Though the travels were long and the people rebellious, He never left them. He stayed with them the entire journey from one side of the wilderness to the other.

It is a given that as long as we live on this earth, we will face times of trial and suffering. For the Christian though, we don't have to go through them alone: God is with us. The peace we feel in the midst of these times is His presence near us. It is His sweet assurance that He is there, walking the journey with us, helping us get to the other side.

"Fear not, for I am with you; be not dismayed, for I am your God; I will strengthen you, I will help you, I will uphold you with my righteous right hand" (Isaiah 41:10 ESV).

Moving Mountains

"The earth is broken up, the earth is split asunder, the earth is violently shaken" (Isaiah 24:19 NIV).

In 2015 Nepal suffered a major earthquake. It was hard to watch the news reports and see the footage of the devastation after it happened. It was hard to imagine that in one moment, many Nepalese lives were changed forever. There was no time to prepare or make plans or even seek shelter. In the aftermath, the people looked so helpless and totally defeated—and who wouldn't be in the face of such destruction?

As I watched one news report, I was struck by a live camera shot of people digging in the rubble, searching with hope for any survivors who may lie beneath it. As I watched, I noticed that although they were standing on a huge mound of dirt, they were digging slowly with tiny little shovels. I know this was necessary to get people out from below the dirt safely; it just looked so devastatingly fruitless next to the mountains of rubble.

While I watched the report, God brought to mind that this is a good example of the plight of humanity. We are helpless in our sins without Him. We can try to offset our bad deeds with good deeds in hopes of getting to heaven, but it is fruitless. All we are doing is moving dirt around from one place to another because we are totally unqualified and incapable of removing it from our lives. Only God can safely and completely remove the huge mountain of sin between us and Himself. He provided the way through His Son; He just awaits our invitation to complete His salvation work in our hearts.

> "Jesus answered, 'I am the way and the truth and the life. No one comes to the Father except through me'" (John 14:6 NIV).

Healthy Emotions

"A time to weep and a time to laugh; a time to mourn and a time to dance" (Ecclesiastes 3:4 NIV).

Emotions are sometimes tricky to handle. They can be strong and uncontainable. Sometimes they seem misplaced or inappropriate, and other times they feel deep and unreachable. Failing to express our emotions can result in an "emotional soup." By that I mean our heart becomes a container of blended together, indistinguishable emotions, which can turn into depression. It is at this point when we may need professional help to work through it.

I have experienced long periods of depression, times when I felt like my emotional logjam was so strong that if unleashed, someone would be hurt and I would be killed in the process. Carrying the unexpressed emotions around inside me severely affected my thinking. I could not trust my own brain, and life became hard to navigate.

While at times emotions seem like curses, they are true gifts from God. They help us process our thoughts, motivate our actions, and enhance our life experiences. Even our negative emotions are necessary to help us experience positive ones. We would never know joy without sadness, peace without anger, trust without betrayal, strength without weakness, and goodness without evil. God blessed us when He gave us emotions, for without them, we'd never know His love or realize our need for His salvation.

> "My soul yearns, even faints, for the courts of the Lord;
> my heart and my flesh cry out for the living God"
> (Psalm 84:2 NIV).

Depression Brain

> "[Elijah] came to a broom bush, sat down under it and
> prayed that he might die. 'I have had enough, Lord,' he
> said. 'Take my life; I am no better than my ancestors'"
> (1 Kings 19:4b NIV).

Depression is a subject that people don't usually like to discuss. Families and friends of a depressed loved one often believe this supposedly sad mood can be changed easily and at will. Those who experience it often feel helpless to overcome it and frustrated with their friends and families who don't seem to understand. Then upon seeking treatment, they face a long process involving many hours of intense therapy and an extended trial-and-error search for effective medication. There is simply no quick fix for depression.

When I suffered from depression, one of the worse symptoms I dealt with was flawed thinking, which I call "depression brain." It caused me to think things made sense when they did not, and thus I made terrible decisions. For some, this flawed thinking left unchecked can lead to suicide. Convinced their loved ones would be better off without them, they end their suffering permanently. However, in reality, their action sentences friends and family to a lifetime of grief, questioning, shame, and self-blame.

As with depression, before becoming Christians, we all suffered with flawed thinking. Until we heard differently, we lived our lives thinking—or at least hoping—that if we lived a good life, we would get into heaven when we died. The truth is, however, we could never be good enough in our own power; we are helpless without Him. It is a sin debt we owed that we could never repay without the gracious, saving work of Jesus. God tasks us with sharing the news of Jesus' salvation work with those who are still lost in this thinking, news that will allow them to know the truth, feel the conviction of the Holy Spirit, and make an informed decision about accepting Jesus as their Lord and Savior.

> "At one time we too were foolish, disobedient, deceived and enslaved by all kinds of passions and pleasures. We lived in malice and envy, being hated and hating one another. But when the kindness and love of God our Savior appeared, he saved us, not because of righteous things we had done, but because of his mercy" (Titus 3:3-5a NIV).

Grieving with Hope

"Blessed are those who mourn, for they will be comforted" (Matthew 5:4 NIV).

Wedding anniversaries are difficult days after losing a spouse. They are tough reminders of a heart-wrenching separation. On my anniversary, I always grieve the memories of the love my husband and I had for each other and mourn the loss of a future together. It is painful to remember those happier days while trying to live without him. My heart still aches within me even though many years have passed since his death.

Grieving is a process that cannot be measured in time or with numbered steps. We can think we are over the grief one day and the next an unexpected reminder will bring it flooding back again. We never know when it will raise its ugly head and steal our joy. Grief does not have to overcome us, however. God offers His comfort through His Holy Spirit who helps us to find hope for our future.

God began to comfort me the moment my husband died. As he breathed his last, I felt heaven open up as the angels took him home. It was strangely peaceful and left me with the assurance that heaven is a very real place. I knew I had walked my husband to the door of heaven where he would finally receive his healing and be in the presence of Jesus.

God is filled with compassion for us and loves us deeply. He feels our grief and pain, and He comforts us with His love and watchful care. He is always faithful to His word, and thus we have the hope of heaven where we will be reunited with our loved ones.

"And I heard a loud voice from the throne saying, 'Look! God's dwelling place is now among the people, and he will dwell with them. They will be his people, and God himself will be with them and be their God. He will wipe every tear from their eyes. There will be no more

11

death or mourning or crying or pain, for the old order of things has passed away.' He who was seated on the throne said, 'I am making everything new!' Then he said, 'Write this down, for these words are trustworthy and true'" (Revelation 21:3-5 NIV).

God's Promise to Me

"I shall not die, but live, and declare the works of the Lord" (Psalm 118:17 KJV).

When my husband was in the midst of his two-year battle with brain cancer, a friend of mine told me that God had given this verse to her to share with me as a promise. She and I were both convinced that this was a promise of my husband's healing, which gave me the hope I desperately needed. From then on, I prayed believing that this cancer battle would soon be over and my husband would live to share his brilliant testimony of healing. Sadly, that is not what happened. He grew worse and passed away at the tender age of thirty-three.

After I had gone through a long grieving process and fought chronic depression for an extended period of time, this verse came to my mind again. At that moment, God spoke to my heart, and I realized this verse was meant for me and not for my husband! So, in the midst of this terrible struggle, God had seen me and was working on a plan for my future. Through writing my devotions and sharing my testimony, I was indeed living and declaring His works.

It is amazing to look back and see all the ways that God has redeemed this awful situation by giving me insight, empathy, and a testimony. He has never left my side through it all, and He's still working and using this experience to share His works with others. It is amazing to be on the other side and to joyfully tell others of God's faithfulness to keep His promises and how He sees us when we feel overlooked and quietly suffer alone.

"'I say this because I know what I am planning for you,' says the Lord. 'I have good plans for you, not plans to hurt you. I will give you hope and a good future'" (Jeremiah 29:11 NCV).

Joy in the Morning

♡

"Weeping may last through the night, but joy comes with the morning" (Psalm 30:5b NLT).

After my husband died, many of my friends would quote this verse and tell me that joy would come again. They meant well, but I couldn't imagine myself ever feeling joyful again. Joy was uncomfortable to me, and it seemed to downplay the seriousness of the loss I had suffered. Sorrow was all I had left of him, and I wasn't eager to let it go.

With God's help though, I have worked hard to overcome much since my husband died, often fighting through heartache, sadness, and an ugly view of God and His love for me. Clearing out the pain allowed room for joy to come into my heart once again. Eventually I realized that my husband would want me to feel joy again. He is no longer suffering, and I should not be in pain, mourning him forever. The best way to honor my husband's memory is to be happy once again.

While I was depressed, my soul craved joy, but my mental and emotional state would not allow it. Now that I am past the sadness and grief, I find that nothing can stop or contain my joy. God was gracious to carry me through some hard times, and He gave me this precious gift when I was ready. Surely it is a small taste of the joy my husband is now experiencing in heaven.

"Now is your time of grief, but I will see you again and you will rejoice, and no one will take away your joy" (John 16:22 NIV).

Standing in the Gap

♡

"Father to the fatherless, defender of widows—this is
God, whose dwelling is holy" (Psalm 68:5 NLT).

For the second half of my childhood, I grew up without a father in
my home. So I did not have a male parental influence in my life
during the years when I was changing in every way possible. While male
relatives and church leaders tried to take on that role for me, it was not
the same. I knew what I was missing.

I heard Psalm 68:5 at one point during those days, and I remember
realizing that I did have a father, my Heavenly Father, who was there in
that role for me. It made me feel special until the thought occurred to
me that since God was always with me, He saw everything I did. I could
not fool Him nor could I hide anything from Him. As a teenager, I most
certainly messed up, and it hurt me to disappoint Him. Yet each time,
He loved and forgave me and stayed with me through it all.

Fast forward fourteen years, and tragically my daughter became
fatherless and I became a widow. Again, this verse came to my mind,
reminding me that my daughter was not fatherless nor was I husbandless.
For a second time in my life, my Heavenly Father stood in the gap for
me. True to His word, He provided for our needs—financially, physically,
spiritually, and emotionally. Moreover, He defended me several times
when I needed Him to do so. For my part in this relationship, not unlike
an earthly wife, I have learned to lean on Him, trusting and relying on
Him for my needs and yielding myself to His leadership. Thankfully, God
is patient and understanding.

The common thread in my experiences is God's love. He has been
there for me because He does not overlook the needs of His children. He
is ever before us and with us. He has never left us on our own, nor will He
ever. We are forever His precious children, and He is our loving Father.

"The Lord will not reject his people; he will not abandon
his special possession" (Psalm 94:14 NLT).

A Hidden Love Note

"Do not be afraid, little flock, for your Father has been pleased to give you the kingdom" (Luke 12:32 NIV).

Nestled between the well-known verses about seeking first the Kingdom of God and storing up treasures in heaven is this small, tender verse. It's only a few words, but it packs a powerful punch.

I love how Jesus called His listeners "little flock." Through this phrase, He speaks of His love for us, His children. Furthermore, He reveals Himself as the Good Shepherd mentioned in the Psalms, the one who watches over, takes care of, and protects the sheep.

I also noticed the word "little" in "little flock," a word which speaks to me of vulnerability. Just as the wolf is never far from the flock, evil seems to constantly be only one click away from wreaking havoc in our lives. We face a daily battle to protect our own minds from this influence as well as the minds and bodies of our children. It is good to know our Good Shepherd, our defender, is watching over us, ready to lend His aid when we call.

Finally, this verse says that God finds joy in sharing His kingdom with us. As our Shepherd, He leads and guides us, His flock, to clean water and to green pastures and keeps guard over us. He provides for us on a daily basis, and it gives Him great pleasure to do so because He loves us.

This short little verse, hidden among well-known treasures, is a sweet little love note to us. Through it, we know we are cherished and watched over by a good and gracious, all-seeing, all-knowing, and all-powerful Shepherd. We would surely be lost without Him.

"I am the good shepherd; I know my sheep and my sheep know me" (John 10:14 NIV).

Let Him Love You

"See what great love the Father has lavished on us, that
we should be called children of God!" (1 John 3:1a NIV).

I very much admire Mother Theresa, not only for her ministry work
but also for her God-given wisdom. One of her quotes especially
meaningful to me concerned discerning the will of God. Her advice to
those seeking discernment was to simply sit and let Jesus love on their
heart.

This advice seems so simple but taking time to meditate is not easy.
In our electronic age, we are not in the habit of sitting still and opening
our minds to God's voice. We would rather fill them with other people's
thoughts and opinions through the media.

Out of curiosity, I decided to give meditation a try one day. I put on
a Christian song and sat down and thought about all the ways that God
has loved me. Then I listened for Him speak to me through His Holy
Spirit. I soon found myself in tears, totally overwhelmed by His love. It
was an awesome moment.

God will honor our efforts when we seek Him with our whole hearts.
He is waiting for us to spend time with Him so He can share His love
and give us the wisdom and understanding we need. We truly have so
much to gain by simply sitting still and letting God love us.

"And I pray that you, being rooted and established in
love, may have power, together with all the Lord's holy
people, to grasp how wide and long and high and deep is
the love of Christ, and to know this love that surpasses
knowledge—that you may be filled to the measure of all
the fullness of God" (Ephesians 3:17b-19 NIV).

A Different Teenage Love

❤

"My command is this: Love each other as I have loved you" (John 15:12 NIV).

One day as my sister, my teenage nephew, and I left from church, my nephew, who was in front of me, suddenly stopped me in my tracks when he fell to his knees, dropping his huge saxophone case and everything else he was holding. Once I recovered from the shock of his falling, I was amazed to see the reason for his actions. He had done so to give a sweet hug to a precious little two-year-old girl who was reaching up to him. I was blessed to watch him wrap his long, lanky arms around her and hold her while they both smiled. It was probably one of the sweetest sights I have seen in a long time.

Later as I thought about it, I realized there were so many other reactions my nephew could have had at that moment which would have been considered typical for a teenager. He could have walked past the little girl and ignored her. He could have patted her mouse-eared pigtails and smiled down at her. He could have acknowledged her and gone about his business. He could have just let her hug his leg. He didn't do any of that because he loved her. When he got down on her level, he showed her respect as a person who, although young and little, was of great value to him.

As I watched the scene, I felt I was witnessing the powerful love of God. Like the preschooler, we were forever separated from God by a huge span of sinfulness, unable to reach Him ourselves no matter how hard we tried. He loved us so much that He made a way for us to be together again by allowing His Son, Jesus, to come down to our level and suffer death to accomplish it. God would have never allowed this to happen if He did not love and value us. Despite the cost to Himself, He does not force us to love Him back because He desires a bond with us that is genuine and reciprocal. He gives us the choice to accept or reject Him and to receive whatever benefits or consequences our choice may bring.

"This is how God showed his love for us: God sent his only Son into the world so we might live through him. This is the kind of love we are talking about—not that we once upon a time loved God, but that he loved us and sent his Son as a sacrifice to clear away our sins and the damage they've done to our relationship with God" (1 John 4:9-10 MSG).

A Healing Touch

"Jesus turned and saw her. 'Take heart, daughter,' he said, 'your faith has healed you.' And the woman was healed at that moment" (Matthew 9:22 NIV).

In Matthew chapter nine, we read of several healings Jesus performed in quick succession. He healed a dying young girl, a chronically ill woman, two blind men, and a mute, demon-possessed man. In all instances, His healing met their faith, and they were made whole.

It is important to note that Jesus didn't look at their illness and write them off as unclean and useless to Him, which would have been a typical response in those days. Rather He saw them as they were, His hurting children who believed He could heal them. He honored their faith by graciously granting their requests.

In our day, we use all kinds of labels to describe people—criminal, homeless, dirty, sick, handicapped, gay, drunk—often using these labels as a reason to shun them. Jesus, our example, however, looked beyond these labels. He looked at their hearts and saw their true need, the need for a healing touch from their merciful and loving Savior.

"The Lord does not look at the things people look at. People look at the outward appearance, but the Lord looks at the heart" (1 Samuel 16:7b NIV).

The Easy Life

"I told you these things so that you can have peace in me. In this world you will have trouble, but be brave! I have defeated the world" (John 16:33 NCV).

When times are tough, it can be hard to get up and face another day. I have many times moaned and groaned about my life in self-imposed pity parties for one. I have often wondered why my life was hard and always a constant struggle. Why was my life full of drama? Why couldn't it be easy?

God tenderly spoke to my heart in reply. He showed me how my life experiences have shaped me into the person I am today and how He has used them to bring me closer to Him. I don't personally believe He caused these traumatic experiences to happen to me, but I do believe He went through them with me.

The truth is I may have never realized my need for God or love Him as deeply as I do now if my life was painless, drama-free, and idyllic. God's victory in my life is my story, and sharing it is my purpose. To wish my life away would be to give up my testimony, the story of God's love for me, and that is something I would never want to give up.

"I pray that Christ will live in your hearts by faith and that your life will be strong in love and be built on love" (Ephesians 3:17 NCV).

What's Your Sign?

ᗢ

"A new command I give you: Love one another. As I
have loved you, so you must love one another. By this
everyone will know that you are my disciples, if you love
one another" (John 13:34-35 NIV).

As I was traveling one day, I noticed a vehicle with a personalized
plate that said, "Greedy." The thought struck me: what would life
would be like if we had to wear labels indicating our faults or our value?
What if we had to walk around in our day-to-day life labeled as *selfish,
liar,* or *thief?* How would people treat us? How would we treat people?
Would we give someone money if they were labeled a thief? Would we
trust someone labeled a liar? Would we share with someone labeled as
selfish?

Thankfully, Jesus did not go by the popular labels and societal roles
of his day. He saw preachers and deacons in fishermen, and missionaries
in Pharisees. He saw value in women and children. He saw redemption
for tax collectors and adulterers. He saw a brighter future for the sick
and disabled.

Everyone Jesus met, including His tormentors, received His love
and grace. He showed us by example how He wants us to love and treat
people, even those we label as "lost causes" or "worthless." Loving others
is not an easy task but one that we have to rely on the power of God to
do through us. Everything is possible when a heart is willing to be used
by our Almighty God.

"Jesus looked at them and said, 'With man this is impossible, but not with God; all things are possible with
God'" (Mark 10:27 NIV).

Death to a Dream

"All of us have become like one who is unclean, and all our righteous acts are like filthy rags; we all shrivel up like a leaf, and like the wind our sins sweep us away" (Isaiah 64:6 NIV).

God has shown me in no uncertain terms that I have to give up on my dream, a dream I didn't realize I had even though I had been working toward it my entire life: the dream of perfectionism. Like many other perfectionistic dreamers, I pressured myself to be the perfect employee, the perfect mother, the perfect housekeeper, the perfect money manager, the perfect church member, and the perfect Christian, and I wanted to achieve it all simultaneously.

This crazy goal came with many strange bedfellows. I felt guilty all the time because I couldn't measure up to my own unrealistic standards. I lived under constant stress from trying to stay in control and balanced at the same time. Caught in a sad, endless cycle, I felt like a failure and unworthy of anyone's approval.

Thankfully, God saved me from myself, gently showing me I was not intended to chase an impossible dream. I can never achieve perfection because only He is sinless (1 John 1:8). Thus, in seeking that perfection, I put myself in bondage to the pursuit.

He also showed me Mark 12:3 in a brand-new way. The second part of His two greatest commandments is "love your neighbor as yourself." If I loved others as much as I loved myself, I would not love others much at all. This lack of love for myself was definitely not what God intended.

In examining my self-imposed goal of perfection, I found freedom. I also discovered something wonderful: my perfect God finds me worthy of His love just as I am, imperfections and all.

"The Lord appeared to him from afar, saying, 'I have loved you with an everlasting love; Therefore I have drawn you with lovingkindness'" (Jeremiah 31:3 NASB).

A Dependent Strength

"I will instruct you and teach you in the way you should go; I will counsel you with my loving eye on you" (Psalm 32:8 NIV).

I took a quiz online one day to determine the kind of woman that I am. While I don't hold stock in these silly, little quizzes, this one interested me. My results showed I was an independent woman. I agree with that result, but it was definitely not a goal I set for myself. It was absolutely by necessity.

I have had to be independent since I was young. As a first-born child in a single-parent home, it was necessary that I help out and take care of my younger sister. As an adult, I found myself on the flip-side, this time in the role of the single parent. I had no choice but to find a way to take care of everything.

Now after living through all that, I look back with amazement at what God has been able to accomplish through me and for me. He invested His grace, mercy, provision, courage, and love in me and made up the difference between what I thought I could do and what I have actually done. He was the glue that held me together and strengthened me.

So in reality, I am not an independent woman; I am a woman who is dependent on God for everything. I am not alone because we all are truly dependent on Him. This dependency is not a liability, however: it is a strength. He turns our weaknesses into strengths and our meager efforts into great accomplishments.

"But he said to me, 'My grace is sufficient for you, for my power is made perfect in weakness.' Therefore I will boast all the more gladly about my weaknesses, so that Christ's power may rest on me" (2 Corinthians 12:9 NIV).

Finding Your Way in the Dark

⟡

"Faith assures us of things we expect and convinces us of the existence of things we cannot see." (Hebrews 11:1 GW).

When I was a freshman in college, a couple of my friends, my boyfriend, and I went to Cumberland Falls together one evening. We decided to walk down to a little beach area a safe distance from the bottom of the falls. We had so much fun we forgot the time and found ourselves in complete darkness without a flashlight. Our friends were locals who were familiar with the park, so they led us as we literally felt our way around the rocks to the parking lot. My eyes never did adjust to the darkness. It was terrifying.

I had only started dating my boyfriend, so I didn't know if I could trust him. We were still trying to impress each other at this point in our relationship. So toward that end, he set out to be my hero, tenderly guiding me and speaking calm reassurances into my ear. At one point he used humor to calm me by saying, "Don't worry, old eagle-eyes will save you!" Next thing I knew, he was lying on the ground! We had a great laugh, relieving the tension for a few moments. Despite our follies, we made it out safely and were able to get back to school before curfew.

It has been said that every journey begins with a first step. Walking our faith journey is no exception. God may ask us to do something we feel is scary and difficult such as walking in darkness. However, He doesn't send us alone; He goes with us. He may not show us the entire map of our journey at one time, but He will light up our path one step at a time as we are ready for it. We can walk confidently with Him because He won't abandon us along the way. He is truly the best traveling companion and tour guide we could ever have with us.

"Be strong and courageous. Don't tremble! Don't be afraid of them! The Lord your God is the one who is

going with you. He won't abandon you or leave you"
(Deuteronomy 31:6 GW).

Listening to God Is No Fluff

$\heartsuit$

"Let the wise listen and add to their learning, and let the
discerning get guidance" (Proverbs 1:5 NIV).

If you are a parent, you have probably had to explain to your child at
least one time the difference between hearing and listening. Hearing
is letting sound go in one ear and out the other, skipping the brain.
However, listening is letting the message register with the brain so a
proper reaction can be offered. It is important for children to learn
this lesson so they can properly respond to others, especially those in
authority over them.

Many children, including my own child, prefer to learn lessons the
hard way. When my daughter was a preschooler, she used to help me do
laundry. Every time she did so, she would argue with me incessantly that
dryer lint was cotton candy. No matter how many times I told her—and
I said it to her every single time—she refused to listen and believe the
truth.

Finally exasperated one day, I told her to go ahead and taste it. I
will never forget the shocked look on her face as she ingested this nasty
fluff. It was a look of disappointment mixed with wounded pride as she
realized it was not cotton candy, and therefore, I was right and she was
wrong. I wanted to spare her this awful experience, but it turned out to
be the only way she finally learned the truth.

Spiritually speaking, listening to God is also a wise practice. However,
it requires active listening on our part, for in order to hear Him, we have
to draw close to Him, and in order to recognize His voice, we have to
learn to listen for it. It is a process, but one worth pursuing if we want
to gain wisdom from God and show Him that we trust and believe Him.

"If any of you lacks wisdom, you should ask God, who gives generously to all without finding fault, and it will be given to you" (James 1:5 NIV).

Do You Hear Me?

"Hear me, my people, and I will warn you—if you would only listen to me, Israel!" (Psalm 81:8 NIV).

I think all children go through a time when they get into the habit of saying, "Huh?" At first it comes from not being able to hear something, but then it becomes a habit. We can recognize it as a habit when they start answering us before we repeat the question, which shows they were just ignoring us. To break them of this habit, we have to stop repeating ourselves when we know they heard us.

Similarly, I wonder how many times we ignore God's voice. We often ask for help and for answers, yet we don't always expectantly listen for His response. Thankfully, He is patient and kind because He probably has to repeat Himself many times to get our attention. Even if we haven't asked Him for anything, I wonder how many blessings we miss because we are not attuned to His voice.

So how do we listen expectantly? A good start is to work on our personal relationship with Him—spend time with Him in prayer, meditation, worship, Bible study, and fellowship. We can furthermore ask Him to make us aware of Him and then attentively wait for that to happen. With practice, we will soon learn to recognize the subtle communications and affirmations from the Holy Spirit as He speaks to our hearts. Our ability to hear God is only limited by our attention span and our willingness to listen.

"Call to me and I will answer you, and will tell you great and hidden things that you have not known" (Jeremiah 33:3 ESV).

Walking in the Way

♡

"Walk in obedience to all that the Lord your God has commanded you, so that you may live and prosper and prolong your days in the land that you will possess" (Deuteronomy 5:33 NIV).

Each morning as I drive to work, I see middle-school students walking to school with their parents. It is often obvious that these students feel they are ready to let go of their parents, but their parents are not ready to let go of them.

One student especially stood out as being particularly embarrassed to have his dad walk him to school. He was head and shoulders taller than his dad, and I could tell that he was aware of that fact and was extremely put out to have his dad walking with him. The son stalwartly looked forward and walked quickly to be done with this horrid walk of shame. His dad, oblivious to what I could clearly see, persistently followed his son, often having to jog to keep up while dodging the tree branches that bounced off his son.

If we are not careful, we can be like this middle-school student in our walk with God. We can become too ashamed, independent, and impatient to walk with Him. Even worse, we can also become rebellious and purposefully decide to walk away from Him.

I hope this student looks back one day and realizes how much he took his dad for granted. This walk of shame, while inconvenient to him, was proof of his dad's love and care. Hopefully, he will realize this before it is too late to thank his dad.

Likewise, we shouldn't take our walk with God for granted either.

How awful it would be to get to the end of our journey and realize everything we missed because we went our own way. Thankfully, God, like this student's father, is undaunted by our attitude and chooses to walk with us the entire way. Fortunately for us too, we still have time to appreciate this journey and the companionship of our most patient and persistent Heavenly Father.

> "Therefore as you have received Christ Jesus the Lord, so walk in Him, having been firmly rooted and now being built up in Him and established in your faith, just as you were instructed, and overflowing with gratitude" (Colossians 2:6-7 NASB).

Walk, Don't Run

> "Mark out a straight path for your feet; stay on the safe path" (Proverbs 4:26 NLT).

I was at the pool one Saturday for an exercise class, and as we finished up, I noticed a little three-year old boy swimming in the smaller pool with his mom and dad. This family was familiar to me because I often see them swimming in the pool together, and I noticed their son taking weekly swimming lessons there for several months.

This particular day, I noticed the little boy was especially rowdy. As his parents talked with friends in the pool, he would get away from them, climb out of the pool, run around it, and then jump back in again. His parents would remind him often to walk so he wouldn't slip on the wet concrete and get hurt. He would slow down and walk like it was excruciatingly painful before taking off running again.

Finally, the inevitable happened, and he slipped and fell down. He whimpered a little bit, but soon got up and started running again while his parents loudly told him to stop. Suddenly his feet completely went out from under him, and he fell hard on his back, smacking his head on the pavement. His parents were by his side in seconds. They held him close while he cried loudly, and they calmly explained to him that this is what happens when he disobediently runs around the pool. Before I knew it though, he was back up and running again.

As I watched this scene play out, I wondered if this is what God goes through with us. We run ahead of Him fearlessly or we lag behind Him fearfully, yet God chooses to encourage us rather than force us to do anything. He is there for us whenever we fall, hoping we will learn from our mistakes. Fortunately for us, God will never give up on us. I hate to imagine where we would be if He did.

> "But Lord, your nurturing love is tender and gentle. You are slow to get angry yet so swift to show your faithful love. You are full of abounding grace and truth" (Psalm 86:15 TPT).

God in Flesh

> "He walks with me and He talks with me, and He tells me I am His own. And the joy we share as we tarry there, none other has ever known."—from the hymn "In the Garden¹"

This is one of my favorite hymns because it makes me think of my grandpa who loved it too. The hymn beautifully speaks of a visit with God where we physically walk and talk together in the garden. We can only imagine it now, but when we are finally able to physically walk with Him and hear His voice, we will realize how satisfying it is and how much we've yearned for it.

Taking this conversation out of the garden though, what would it be like if He physically walked and talked to us through a random day of our life? What if we could physically see Him listening to our conversations, witnessing our actions and decisions, and watching TV or scrolling the internet with us?

As much as we love Jesus, I'm sure it would be a stressful and nerve-wracking day. We would try to live the perfect Christian life doing everything we should do and trying not to do anything we shouldn't. However, since we are not perfect in word or deed, we would probably have to seek His forgiveness at least once by the end of that day.

Even though Jesus is not physically beside us each day, He is with us spiritually each moment. He does walk and talk with us, and He does see and hear our hearts. Thankfully though, He is full of grace and forgiveness, which He freely grants when we seek it with all our hearts.

> "In him we have redemption through his blood, the forgiveness of sins, in accordance with the riches of God's grace that he lavished on us" (Ephesians 1:7-8 NIV).

The Golden Rule

> "So in everything, do to others what you would have them do to you, for this sums up the Law and the Prophets" (Matthew 7:12 NIV).

The Golden Rule, stated in Matthew 7:12, is a rule many of us grew up with as we learned how to get along with other people. We were not born with an innate respect for the feelings of others. Thus, it had to be taught to us and practiced daily.

When I was a young pastor's wife, I decided to reverse it and treat people the way they treated me. It sounded like a good plan at the time, especially when dealing with difficult people in the church. However, while the plan may have been good in theory, it didn't work out as I had thought. I soon discovered that people did not appreciate being treated the way they treated others, and they were stunned by the way I acted. The truth is, it didn't do anyone any good, and it just gave me the excuse to be rude and difficult to rude and difficult people. I learned that God wanted me to shape my attitude according to His commands and not to the actions of others.

The last part of Nehemiah 5:15, which is printed below, drove the point home to me. Our attitudes are a reflection of our heart and where we stand in our relationship with God. When Jesus was on earth, He treated others respectfully, making them feel loved and valued. So out of reverence for Him, we should also treat people with love and respect, for in this way, we honor God's command and reflect His love to others.

"But out of reverence for God I did not act like that" (Nehemiah 5:15b NIV).

Transforming into His Likeness

"And so we are transfigured much like the Messiah, our lives gradually becoming brighter and more beautiful as God enters our lives and we become like Him" (2 Corinthians 3:18 MSG).

I think it is interesting to observe how twins and close siblings interact with each other. Some talk over one another and answer a question using the exact same words. My sister and I are able to look at each other and break out in hysterical laughter without even saying a word because we know each other that well.

I have also noticed that longtime married couples often become like one person, taking on each other's mannerisms, having their particular ways of doing things, and developing their own way of communicating. They may even start to look and dress alike.

Much like these close relationships, we should spend so much time with Jesus that people see Him when they look at us. The more time we spend with Him, the more like Him we will become. He will light up our lives with His presence and we will reflect His love-light on others. We then become His beacon of hope and salvation, drawing the lost out of the darkness of sin and into His wonderful light.

> "But in your hearts revere Christ as Lord. Always be prepared to give an answer to everyone who asks you to give the reason for the hope that you have" (1 Peter 3:15a NIV).

A Lasting Impression

> "Therefore be imitators of God, as beloved children. And walk in love, as Christ loved us and gave himself up for us, a fragrant offering and sacrifice to God" (Ephesians 5:1-2 ESV).

I was in a gym locker room one day and overheard some comments a group of ladies were making about another woman:

"I just love Elizabeth."

"I don't know what it is about her, but I feel joyful whenever I am with her."

"You know that she genuinely cares about you when you are with her."

"She makes me feel better about myself."

"She makes me feel calm."

I didn't know Elizabeth, but she certainly sounded like a Christian to me. I was so impressed with this woman that I took time to evaluate the type of impression I left on people. I sincerely hoped that people saw me as they saw Elizabeth.

Whether she intended to or not, Elizabeth imitated Jesus with her actions. We are all called to do likewise. Jesus treated people with kindness and loved people powerfully. This amazing, unconditional love is still active and changing lives today, thanks to people like Elizabeth who beautifully share it with others.

"May the words of my mouth and the meditation of my heart be pleasing to you, O Lord, my rock and my redeemer" (Psalm 19:14 NLT).

Measuring Up

"The Lord your God has blessed you in all the work of your hands. He has watched over your journey through this vast wilderness. These forty years the Lord your God has been with you, and you have not lacked anything" (Deuteronomy 2:7 NIV).

Life is a marathon, not a sprint. How many times have we heard this saying? I know I heard it often, especially when I was a young adult. I was like an impatient and spoiled child wanting the "perfect life" instantly. I wanted the house in the suburbs, the nice car, the good job, and the husband and family. What I didn't realize was that those people whose lives I coveted had worked a lifetime to achieve what I wanted. I did not see all the hardships and years of struggle they went through to get there.

I think it is the same in the Christian life. We look at the faith-walk of older, polished Christians and think we are failures because we are not as strong and faithful as they are. We forget they have a history which we can't see. They also struggled and tried and failed in their Christian walk. They spent countless hours in prayer, Bible study, and worship, fine-tuning their walk with God. All these experiences were used by God to increase their faith, deepen their relationship with Him, and shape them into the Christians we see them as today.

Ironically though, I venture to guess that many of these saints do not see themselves as the strong, faithful Christians we perceive them to be. They probably still see themselves struggling in pursuit of that goal. They know they are not through; they are still running the marathon with us.

No matter where we are in our walk with God, we all push toward that finish line together, the finish line paved in heavenly gold and lined on either side by the cheering saints whose Christian walk led us heavenward.

> "Therefore we do not lose heart. Though outwardly we are wasting away, yet inwardly we are being renewed day by day. For our light and momentary troubles are achieving for us an eternal glory that far outweighs them all. So we fix our eyes not on what is seen, but on what is unseen, since what is seen is temporary, but what is unseen is eternal" (2 Corinthians 4:16-18 NIV).

Getting in the Way

> "I am the Lord your God who brought you up out of the land of Egypt. Open your mouth wide and I will fill it" (Psalm 81:10 NIV).

Every day when I get home from work, my cats greet me at the door. I'm not sure if they are happy to see me or just excited to get their dinner. Once I get through the door, we all proceed to dance. I attempt to walk up the stairs and into the kitchen while the cats wind around my ankles. They do so to show affection and to rub their scent glands on me, making sure the other non-existent cats know I, the person with the food, belong to them. As they do this, I get their food and their dishes, put the food into their dishes, and put the dishes on the floor while simultaneously trying not to step on a paw or a tail. Unfortunately,

I'm not always successful at it, but that doesn't stop them from doing it again the next day.

I have often wondered if this is how we are with God. He longs and waits to pour out blessings upon us, and our lack of faith and trust prevents Him from easily doing so. Sometimes we stubbornly choose to go our own way or refuse to seek His will and direction. Other times we become fearful of the journey and refuse to be moved. As a result, our fear and stubbornness prohibit us from fully experiencing the life God intended for us.

Like my cats, if we would step back and evaluate the situation, we might see the truth. My cats would get fed a lot faster and with less risk of harm if they simply waited by their food dishes. Perhaps we would inherit blessings sooner and more abundantly if we would get out of God's way and expectantly wait on Him. I wonder how many times we've had to wait longer because we failed to trust Him sooner.

> "The Lord is near to all who call on him, to all who call on him in truth. He fulfills the desires of those who fear him; he hears their cry and saves them" (Psalm 145:18-19 NIV).

My Pleasure

> "Enter his gates with thanksgiving and his courts with praise; give thanks to him and praise his name" (Psalm 100:4 NIV).

During the Thanksgiving season, we often feel challenged to express our gratitude for our blessings. Toward this end, many of my friends take part in the challenge to post something they are grateful for on social media each day in November. It is a good exercise in practicing gratitude.

Whenever I think of thankfulness and gratitude, I instantly think of the famous chicken restaurant who has their employees respond to customers' thanks by saying, "My pleasure." It seems like such a small gesture, but it is a powerful phrase, which makes customers feel as if they are being served by employees who are genuinely glad to serve them. The franchise hopes this phrase will encourage their employees to smile and give good customer service, leaving the customers feeling special, appreciated, and important so they will want to come back again.

As demonstrated by these employees, we are also to serve the Lord with pleasure, gladness, and thanksgiving. God enjoys genuine, wholehearted worship and service which flow from hearts full of gratitude and love. I can just imagine as we pour out our thankful hearts to Him that He looks upon us with eyes full of kindness, pride, and love, and quietly whispers, "Child, it was My pleasure."

> "Fear not, little flock, for it is your Father's good pleasure to give you the kingdom" (Luke 12:32 ESV).

What's in a Name?

> "The gatekeeper opens the gate for him, and the sheep listen to his voice. He calls his own sheep by name and leads them out" (John 10:3 NIV).

Sometimes when I am home on vacation, I attend a stretching and relaxation water class at the gym. I don't go often so I had a hard time getting to know the people in the class. That suddenly changed one day, however, when a lady I hardly knew said hello to me and called me by name. I was amazed at how her use of my name instantly made me feel important and a part of the group.

It reminded me of a story a pastor friend told about a guest's experience at church. The pastor knew the guest was coming, so he alerted the door greeters and told them where to direct him. Then when the guest arrived, the greeters met him, recognized his name, and took him where he needed to go. He later told the pastor that he felt welcomed instantly and was surprised that so many people knew his name.

Our names are one of the most personal and individual aspects about us. So when people use our name, they convey the message that they cared enough to remember us personally. This individual touch can be the catalyst to transform an acquaintanceship into a friendship.

Jesus tells us in John 10:3 that He knows our names. Think about it: there are billions of people on this planet, and He knows each of us by name—first, middle, maiden, last, nickname, and so on. Moreover, the Bible tells us that He knew us before we even knew ourselves (Jeremiah 1:4-5); He knows how many tears we have cried (Psalm 56:8) and how many hairs are on our heads (Luke 12:7). He knows all this because we are His beloved masterpieces.

He calls us by our names because He doesn't want to just be acquainted with us: He wants to be our dearest, most trusted, and faithful friend.

> "For we are God's workmanship, created in Christ Jesus to do good works, which God prepared in advance as our way of life" (Ephesians 2:10 BSB).

Becoming Part of the Solution

> "Another of his disciples, Andrew, Simon Peter's brother, spoke up, 'Here is a boy with five small barley loaves and two small fish, but how far will they go among so many?'" (John 6:8-9 NIV).

Previous to the story from which this verse was taken, the disciples had just returned from a mission trip (Luke 9:1-10). They had been asked by Jesus to go from village to village healing people and telling them about Him. They were not to take any bread or money, only relying on the kindness of strangers.

When they got back, Jesus saw their need for rest and sought a quiet place for them. The crowds, however, followed them. Late in the day, the crowd became hungry, and the disciples asked Jesus to send the people away to get a meal. Jesus instead asked the disciples to feed them. Despite the fact that the disciples had just experienced great miracles of healing and provision for themselves, they argued about how to feed the multitudes of people.

Andrew, however, who seemed to frequently bring people to Jesus, brought attention to a young boy who was willing to share his meager lunch. Jesus accepted this gift. He sat the people down and blessed the little lunch, and the disciples gave it out to the people. The food multiplied, and there were twelve baskets left over, enough to give each disciple a basketful.

Andrew stands out in this story because while others were stressed, searching for answers, he brought Jesus an opportunity. In so doing, he became part of the solution rather than the problem. The same could be said of David when he offered to fight Goliath. While his brothers and fellow soldiers were caught in a standoff with the giant and his army, David volunteered to fight the giant himself. God blessed both Andrew and David for their willingness by involving them in a mighty way, impacting many lives for generations.

In our modern world, people still search for hope and help in dealing with both serious and everyday problems. We take part in God's solution when we offer up our means, our time, and our energy to sacrificially meet their needs in the name of Jesus. Hopefully, they will be willing to listen to what we have to say after we have shown them God's love through our actions.

> "Instead, you must worship Christ as Lord of your life. And if someone asks about your hope as a believer, always be ready to explain it" (1 Peter 3:15 NLT).

A Seat in the Lifeboat

"For God so loved the world that he gave his one and only Son, that whoever believes in him shall not perish but have eternal life" (John 3:16 NIV).

I am not a huge history buff, but I enjoy the personal side of history, especially reading firsthand accounts of those who witnessed historical events. I once read an interesting article concerning a letter written by a French woman who survived the Titanic disaster. In her letter, she graphically described the confusion and raw emotion of the people during and after the disaster.

The article was moving, but what touched me the most was a reader's comment speaking of the heroism of the men who loaded the women and children into the lifeboats. Basically, the reader said that every time these men put a person in a lifeboat, they must have realized they were lowering their own chance for survival. Repeatedly sacrificing their life for another must have been agonizing.

Jesus made such a sacrifice when He put our lives in front of His own as He became the sacrifice for our sins. The Bible says that before His arrest, Jesus suffered as He passionately prayed in the garden. In his humanity, He must have been feeling the emotions of a man about to die, but as our God, His love compelled Him to endure the pain in order to provide us a way to salvation. In so doing, He gave us eternal life at the cost of His own, providing us with a seat in His lifeboat.

"For Christ also suffered once for sins, the righteous for the unrighteous, to bring you to God. He was put to death in the body but made alive in the Spirit" (1 Peter 3:18 NIV).

A Powerful Lesson

"But you will receive power when the Holy Spirit comes on you; and you will be my witnesses in Jerusalem, and in all Judea and Samaria, and to the ends of the earth" (Acts 1:8 NIV).

I have co-taught a women's Bible study group for years, and even though I've done it for a long time, I still struggle with every lesson I teach. For me, teaching an adult class is both intimidating and humbling. I get stuck in my head very easily and overthink the situation. I question myself, "Who am I to teach anyone? Surely they know more than I do." Then I wrestle with how to make the lesson meaningful and interesting both to people who have been in church for years and to those who are new in their faith. All these issues are multiplied by my underlying fear of talking in front of people, especially people I don't know.

A friend recently told me how amazed she was that I could teach an adult class since I was shy, anxious, and introverted. She said it revealed the work of God in my life. In that moment, God used her comments to bring the Holy Spirit's power to my mind.

Before ascending into heaven, Jesus told the disciples that the Holy Spirit would come upon them and they would be His witnesses. Several days later on the day we know as Pentecost, the Holy Spirit powerfully filled the disciples and empowered them to boldly preach the Word to multitudes of people and to do so in languages they didn't actually know. Many people were saved that day, and the church suddenly grew exponentially.

From this story, I realized the reason I struggled was because I was trying to teach *about* God and not *with* God. He is the one who can give me courage and a meaningful way to teach, as well as the lesson He wants the ladies to hear. Without Him, Bible study is merely a social club, a moral debate, or a history lesson. His presence and power make all the difference.

"Jesus looked hard at them and said, 'No chance at all if you think you can pull it off by yourself. Every chance in the world if you trust God to do it'" (Matthew 19:26 MSG).

Believing Is Seeing

$\heartsuit$

"Immediately, something like scales fell from Saul's eyes, and he could see again. He got up and was baptized" (Acts 9:18 NIV).

Poor eyesight runs in my family on both sides. It is pretty much inevitable that each of us will have to have glasses. In fact, most of us have had to wear glasses from the time we were in grade school. I remember getting my first pair. When I put them on, everything suddenly shifted from fuzzy to crystal clear. I could distinguish colors, read the teacher's blackboard, and watch television from a distance. I didn't realize how bad my eyesight was until I saw sharp, distinguishable, and vividly colored images for the first time.

I think this is a good description of the difference between living by faith and living by sight, as mentioned in 2 Corinthians 5:7. We can't always trust our physical eyesight when we look at our circumstances, especially when we are going through a hard time, because God does not always work the way we think He should, and we can't always see what He is doing. We want Him to work in A, B, C order when He's on a whole different, secretly-coded alphabet. Through our physical eyes, our outlook may seem bleak, blurry, and hopeless, but our perception is skewed because we are not seeing clearly.

If we look at our circumstances through glasses of faith, however, we trust that no matter how bad life looks, God is working it out for us. Our faith-filled hearts believe that God in His goodness has our best interest in mind. We trust that He will make a way for us to overcome our circumstances, and we will be blessed in knowing that it was His work on our behalf that made it all possible. When all is said and done, we will want to give Him the praise and glory that He most definitely deserves and will want to tell others all about His goodness.

> "Trust in the Lord with all your heart, and do not lean on your own understanding. In all your ways acknowledge him, and he will make straight your paths" (Proverbs 3:5-6 ESV).

Perceiving Reflections

> "Now all we can see of God is like a cloudy picture in a mirror. Later we will see him face to face. We don't know everything, but then we will, just as God completely understands us" (1 Corinthians 13:12 CEV).

One of my girlfriends told me about a poll that was taken about how men and women look in a mirror. She said that the results showed that on average women look into a mirror seventeen times a day, and men look into a mirror twenty-two times a day. Furthermore, when women look into the mirror, they look at the parts of the body they don't like about themselves, and men concentrate on the parts they do like about themselves.

This outcome is surprising to me, but it shows how we see life differently. We each see the world through a variety of lenses shaped by our culture, history, emotions, families, friends, spirituality, education, and so much more. Therefore, we can all look at a single reflected image and each interpret it differently.

As Christians, when we look at ourselves against our standard, God's Word, we may not like what we see. When God looks at us through His eyes of grace, however, He sees His beautiful children living in a fallen world. The condition of our hearts is of utmost concern to Him. After all, our God paid a high price for the redemption of our souls, and He is looking to see what we did with His precious gift, namely, His Son, Jesus Christ.

> "But the Lord said to Samuel, 'Do not consider his appearance or his height, for I have rejected him. The Lord does not look at the things people look at. People look at the outward appearance, but the Lord looks at the heart'" (1 Samuel 16:7 NIV).

The Gift of Failure

> "For the moment all discipline seems painful rather than pleasant, but later it yields the peaceful fruit of righteousness to those who have been trained by it" (Hebrews 12:11 ESV).

One of the hardest lessons I learned as a parent was teaching my child how to deal with failure. Like most parents, I did not want my child to fail, and my child did not want to fail either. However, I realized that by not allowing her to do so, I ran the risk of her becoming perfectionistic, fearful to try new things, over-confident, or reliant upon success to measure her self-worth. I also realized that allowing her to fail as a child in my care was much better than sending her out into the adult world unequipped to deal with adult-sized, more serious failures.

When we allow our children to make mistakes on their own, they learn how to overcome them. They learn not to take failure personally, but to take it as a step toward success. They learn confidence, self-worth, and courage, and we get opportunities to teach them how to rely on God.

We, as maturing Christians, can also get stuck in the fear of failure. We can become so afraid of failing or letting God and others down that we refuse to take any risks. We won't go on a mission trip, teach a Sunday School class, work in the nursery, or attempt anything new. However, without taking risks, we miss out on the hope of anticipation, the joy of success, and the opportunity for growth and blessings. As a consequence, we can live unfulfilled, hopeless Christian lives.

It helps to know that when we do fail, we don't fail alone. God is not only in our successes but also in our failures. We grow in faith through our failures by watching God turn them around for our benefit and for His glory.

Peter denied Jesus three times out of fear, but through the restoration process, he learned how deeply Jesus loved him, and he grew more confident in his faith and courageous in his fight against fear. As a result, Peter became a powerful early church leader who followed Christ to his own death on a cross. Peter exemplified how God uses our failures to fuel our successes.

> "The steps of a man are established by the Lord, when he delights in his way; though he fall, he shall not be cast headlong, for the Lord upholds his hand" (Psalm 37:23-24 ESV).

He Remembers

> "But God remembered Noah and all the wild animals and the livestock that were with him in the ark, and he sent a wind over the earth, and the waters receded" (Genesis 8:1 NIV).

Sometimes when we are in the midst of a trial, we wonder if God forgets us. We pray urgently and persistently, hoping for our answer to come quickly. Then when God doesn't respond immediately, we can become discouraged and wonder if He is still there and if He cares.

There are many verses like Genesis 8:1 above which mention God remembering. These verses seem to imply that God forgets, but nothing can be further from the truth. The Bible plainly says in Isaiah 49:15b-16 that God will not forget us because we are engraved on the palms of His hands. The Bible also assures us in Hebrews 13:5 that He will never leave us or forsake us. The phrase "God remembered" actually means that God decided the time was right to act on someone's behalf.

While it may seem as if He has abandoned us, we need to remind ourselves that He's still there, but we may not see Him working. We can get tunnel vision looking for God to answer the way we want Him to at the exclusion of all else. If we pray for God to show us His work and look for it, we will see it.

No matter how bad our life-storms get, we can be certain that we are not forgotten or alone. God loves us more than we understand, so much so that we are not only engraved in the palms of His hands but also in the nail-shaped scars on Jesus' hands as well.

> "For I, the Lord your God, hold your right hand; it is I who say to you, 'Fear not, I am the one who helps you'" (Isaiah 41:13 ESV).

Shifting Our Focus

> "And let us run with perseverance the race marked out for us, fixing our eyes on Jesus, the pioneer and perfecter of faith" (Hebrews 12:1b-2a NIV).

My daughter loves to juggle. One day she decided she was going to learn how, so she got a how-to book and spent hours trying to learn. I remember this process vividly because she practiced constantly for days. There would a few minutes of silence followed by several loud thuds and a few ouches, and then she'd start all over again. By the time she learned, she was bruised from head to toe but excited to have developed a new skill which she was able to use in several Christian ministries.

Throughout my daughter's training and later in watching her train others to juggle, I heard her say numerous times that the key for jugglers is to keep their eyes focused on the area in front of them where the balls are at their highest point. If jugglers have to look at their hands, they should use their peripheral vision because by turning their head, they will lose focus and lose the rhythm. It is much easier to focus on one area and trust their hands to catch the balls than to focus on so many moving parts successfully at the same time.

Her instructions are a wonderful life lesson. Often in life, we feel overwhelmed and exhausted from juggling our tasks and responsibilities. Like my daughter said, the problem is our focus. We can't focus on everything at one time, so we should fix our eyes on the highest point, and that point is the Lordship of Jesus Christ. To make Him Lord of our lives, we have to willingly submit ourselves to Him, and that includes our time, our resources, our responsibilities, and so on. Our lives then become all about Him and not about us. In changing our focus, we put God on the throne of our hearts and give Him room to manage the many facets of our lives.

"Trust in the Lord with all your heart and lean not on your own understanding; in all your ways submit to him, and he will make your paths straight" (Proverbs 3:5-6 NIV).

Magnifying God

"O magnify the Lord with me, and let us exalt his name together" (Psalm 34:3 KJV).

Since I have been preparing projected slides for worship services, I have paid more attention to the lyrics, coming to appreciate their beautiful phrasing and deep meanings. Old songs have become new for me again.

Often while I work on the slides, God uses what I read to speak to me. One week, He kept drawing me to the word "magnify." Though it was a familiar word, I found myself questioning how it applies to God. What does it mean to magnify God? How do we magnify God?

The first thing I thought of was a magnifying glass, a helpful tool which makes objects easier to see. This glass makes objects appear larger and reveals intricate details. Like the magnifying glass, when we magnify God, we make it easier for people to see Him. We highlight His goodness and illuminate His love to them.

Secondly, I thought of the word "magnet" as it has the same root word *magna*, which means "great." Magnets have strong pulling power, and when used correctly, they attract metal or other magnets to themselves. When we magnify the Lord, we make Him attractive and appealing, drawing people to Him like the power of the magnet. However, if we magnify an unpleasant picture of God, we can repel people like mismatched magnets.

We are called upon to magnify God to the world around us by showing His great love through our lives. Hopefully, our testimony and our lifestyle will draw others to God and will move them to make Jesus their Savior and Lord.

> "Therefore be imitators of God, as beloved children. And walk in love, as Christ loved us and gave himself up for us, a fragrant offering and sacrifice to God" (Ephesians 5:1-2 ESV).

Consequences of Perceptions

> "There is no fear in love. But perfect love drives out fear, because fear has to do with punishment. The one who fears is not made perfect in love" (1 John 4:18 NIV).

I read an article that said every cognition has its consequence. The word "cognition" means perception, impression, or way of thinking.

So basically, this statement means the way we look at life and respond to it has consequences. This idea is also true for our personal relationships with God, for the way we perceive God's character is the way that we will see His work in our lives. If we perceive Him to be angry, manipulative, and judgmental, we will see His deeds as punishments. If we perceive Him to be loving, we will see His acts as merciful and gracious. If we are confused about our perception of Him, we will struggle to make sense of everything happening around us.

Our perception of God will also affect the way we serve Him and treat others. We can serve out of fear of judgment and retribution or out of love and appreciation. We can walk on eggshells, trying to be perfect so we don't upset Him, or we can try to do our best out of love and appreciation for His giving us the opportunity. We can sit in judgment over other people's sins because we believe that is how God sees them, or we can treat others with love and grace because we believe that is the way God has treated us.

Personally, my view of God has changed over time for the better. I grew up in the age of preachers who seemed to constantly stress the wrath of God, and I believed them. Thus, my lifetime of trauma played into my belief that God was angry and constantly punishing me. God, however, graciously and tenderly worked to show me that He was not being mean to me, but rather He was helping me and loving me through my traumas. As a result, my whole perception of God and my outlook on life totally changed.

Now, I obey Him because I know He loves me and is working things out for my good and because I love Him and don't want to disappoint Him. I love others to the best of my ability because my soul overflows with His love and forgiveness. I no longer tremble in fear of imperfection because I know God can achieve great things through me despite my missteps. I am no longer a sinner in the hands of an angry God; I am a child walking hand in hand with her loving Father.

> "And I will be your Father, and you will be my sons and daughters, says the Lord Almighty" (2 Corinthians 6:18 NLT).

Gracious and Merciful God

"But in your great mercy you did not put an end to them or abandon them, for you are a gracious and merciful God" (Nehemiah 9:31 NIV).

Our God is described as being rich in mercy, meaning He chooses to grant us grace and forgiveness when we do not deserve it. Let's face it: looking at the world in its present state in comparison to God's holiness, if it were not for God's great and compassionate mercy, we would be wiped off the face of the earth and doomed to eternal death for our sins. We are definitely blessed that God is so merciful.

To truly appreciate His mercy, we need to look at how the Bible describes it to us: God's mercy is timely (Hebrews 4:16), never fails and is new every morning (Lamentations 3:22-23), follows us all the days of our lives (Ps. 23:6), is great (2 Samuel 24:14), always protects us (Psalm 40:11), and triumphs over judgment (James 2:13). Furthermore, the Word says that because of His mercy, He provides us a way of escape from temptation (1 Corinthians 10:13) and eternal death (Romans 5:8, Titus 3:3-5), and we can confidently approach His throne without fear (Hebrews 4:16).

We owe a great deal of gratitude to God for His mercy. We have both our physical life and our eternal life because of it, and we also have a rich, personal relationship with our most holy God. What does He ask from us in return for this great gift? He asks us to grant mercy and forgiveness to others just as He has granted them to us (Luke 6:36 and Matthew 18:21-35). Exhibiting these godly attributes to others seems like the least we can do in response to all that He has done for us.

"Like the rest, we were by nature deserving of wrath. But because of his great love for us, God, who is rich in mercy, made us alive with Christ even when we were dead in transgressions—it is by grace you have been saved" (Ephesians 2:3b-5 NIV).

The Humility Tree

"He will not let your foot slip—he who watches over you will not slumber" (Psalm 121:3 NIV).

Whenever the weather gets windy, I think about my visit to the home of one of my former pastors who had built a beautiful cabin on a little knoll in the mountains. He had a special type of lumber brought in from his family's farm in Alabama, and he and his wife literally built this cabin with their own hands. It was beautiful with large picture windows from which to admire the view.

They asked the church staff over for dinner not too long after they moved in. During our visit, a storm started brewing and through the window I noticed a large, limbless tree swaying back and forth wildly. It scared me because it seemed close enough to fall on the house. So I asked the pastor why he hadn't cut the tree down. He said he was planning to but hadn't got to it yet. He said for now it was his "humility tree," a reminder to him that all that he has belongs to God, and without His protection, it could all be gone in a moment.

While I don't agree with putting oneself in danger like that, I do agree with the pastor's truth. It is humbling to know that without the provision of God, we would have nothing. Furthermore, without God's protection, who knows what dangers we might have faced? Since we don't always see His interference and His hand of protection at work in our lives, only He really knows what He's done to protect us.

Despite the dangers and the great unknowns of life, we can have peace and comfort in knowing God is working for us and never needs a moment's rest. He is all-knowing, all-seeing, and all-powerful, yet loves us more than we know and is willing to grant us grace and forgiveness when we mess up. I don't know about you, but that truth is my "humility tree." No matter how much I waver in my trust and faith, God keeps me rooted and planted with His truth.

"The Lord will keep you from all harm—he will watch over your life; the Lord will watch over your coming and going both now and forevermore" (Psalm 121:7-8 NIV).

His Wisdom Is Precious

"[Wisdom] cannot be bought with the finest gold, nor can its price be weighed out in silver" (Job 28:15 NIV).

Several years ago when my husband was terminally ill, I lost my wedding ring. I was totally heartsick. Worse still, I couldn't even pinpoint where or when I had lost it. I just knew that it was precious to me and more so since my husband had terminal cancer. I looked everywhere for it in the house, and then I searched outside with a metal detector. I searched and searched until I ran out of places to look. Then one day after I had given up hope, I glanced down at the floor and saw it under my dresser. It simply appeared, and I was so happy and incredibly thankful to God for helping me find it. My ring was not extravagant or expensive, but it was valuable to me for the love and commitment it symbolized.

God equated His wisdom to a precious jewel, one that we cherish and protect. We need His wisdom because it is infinitely better than ours because our decisions are usually based on emotions, circumstantial evidence, past experiences, and future dreams. However, God's wisdom is not bound by these influences. God is able to see our past, present, and future, and He sees important matters we cannot see. He also knows us well—our history, talents, abilities, and gifts—and therefore knows what is best for us. His wisdom is infallible, and therefore, it is trustworthy. All of these facets make His wisdom precious to us.

God wants what is best for us and loves us immeasurably. We are truly blessed to have Him in our lives. Wisdom and truth are His treasures, and when we passionately seek them as we would a lost wedding ring, He will graciously share them with us.

"God understands the way to [wisdom] and he alone knows where it dwells, for he views the ends of the earth and sees everything under the heavens" (Job 28:23 NIV).

He Makes All Things New

$\heartsuit$

"He who was seated on the throne said, 'I am making everything new!' Then he said, 'Write this down, for these words are trustworthy and true'" (Rev. 21:5 NIV).

One of my favorite stories of an object lesson gone wrong involves an experiential lesson my daughter planned for a college worship service. It was based on her favorite mantra, "God makes things new." When she heard people say something about God working things out for our good, she would usually add, "He makes things new."

At the beginning of this service, the worship team was to give the audience a piece of paper and ask them to anonymously write down any sins or areas of their lives they would like to confess or turn over to God. When finished, they were to fold the paper and put it in a glass vase. Unbeknownst to the audience, the paper was actually flash paper. After everyone had put their paper in the vase, one of the worship team members was supposed to set the paper on fire, which would then flash suddenly as it burned the paper. Then another team member was to take the ashes and write out, "He makes me new."

This plan was all good in theory, but it didn't exactly happen that way. Even though they cleared it with the church staff and the Fire Marshall beforehand, they still nearly had a disaster on their hands. The paper was too much for the small glass vase, and thus when lit, the vase acted as a conduit and the fire shot up in a flaming pillar. It singed the hair of the girl who lit it, and it came close to setting the ceiling of the church basement on fire. The flaming pillar of fire consumed all the paper, then extinguished, leaving no ashes to use to write the message.

The audience didn't know what was supposed to happen, however, and despite the failed attempt, they were still impressed. My daughter said the invitation was sung more passionately than ever that night.

The team had one idea in mind, but God had another. While the team wanted ashes, God wanted total destruction. All He left was a scorched vase as evidence that something miraculous had happened: the total forgiveness of sin by the Most Holy God.

> "Come now, let us settle the matter,' says the Lord. 'Though your sins are like scarlet, they shall be as white as snow; though they are red as crimson, they shall be like wool'" (Isaiah 1:18 NIV).

Lukewarm Christians

> "I know your deeds, that you are neither cold nor hot. I wish you were either one or the other! So, because you are lukewarm—neither hot nor cold—I am about to spit you out of my mouth" (Revelation 3:15-16 NIV).

One morning I woke up to snow. It was trash day, so I decided to bundle up and take my trash out before getting ready for work so I wouldn't get my work clothes wet and dirty. When I was finished, I had worked up a sweat. So I decided to take a cold shower instead of my usual hot, steamy one.

In that moment, as I thought about my shower temperature, this verse about lukewarmness suddenly came to my mind. I thought about the theological explanations of the hot and cold qualities which I've heard many times. I was taught that churches or people who are hot are said to be devoted to God and passionately fervent in their faith and their ministry. Conversely, those who are cold are passionless in their faith and ministry. As bad as that sounds, God said He detests lukewarmness even more.

Oddly enough, I had an epiphany in the shower. I put all these thoughts together with the cool water of the shower, and I realized that lukewarmness is comfortable. If the water is lukewarm, it is not scalding or freezing our skin. It is just the right temperature; it is comfortable.

Applying this idea to the scripture, I thought maybe God doesn't want us to get lukewarm in our faith because then it will be comfortable, possibly leading to boredom, stagnant growth, and a lackadaisical attitude. A lukewarm Christian doesn't feel an immediate need for God and probably only cares to approach Him when the need arises. There is no growth or passion or relationship, just status quo.

God wants and deserves so much more than our spare time and afterthoughts. His love for us cost Him dearly. It caused His Son to leave the comfort of heaven in order to come to earth and suffer excruciating pain while dying on a wooden cross for us. That is a passionate love, and it warrants our wholehearted love, gratitude, and devotion even if it makes us uncomfortable.

> "He has shown you, O mortal, what is good. And what does the Lord require of you? To act justly and to love mercy and to walk humbly with your God" (Micah 6:8 NIV).

A Place to Belong

> "You shall not oppress a stranger, since you yourselves know the feelings of a stranger, for you also were strangers in the land of Egypt" (Exodus 23:9 NASB).

Some years ago, I was searching for a place to belong at my church. I was a young, widowed mother who yearned for other Christian women with whom to do life. I didn't seem to fit in anywhere. So I would sit alone in my car during Sunday School while my daughter attended her youth class.

Then one day, a friend agreed to co-teach a women's class with me. We originally designed the class for women who came alone to church, but it eventually grew and reached out to other women. Now it is a successful class for women, both married and single, younger and older. It has been a real blessing in my life and the lives of other women.

While my story had a good outcome, I don't ever want to forget how I felt sitting in my car alone in the church parking lot. That memory gives me a little taste of what it feels like to be excluded, and thus I am more sympathetic to others who may feel that way.

Have you ever thought about people who may not feel welcomed into your church? Have you ever thought about inviting people to church but worried they would not be welcomed? Have you seen these people in your church lately—the mentally or physically handicapped, the homosexual, the addict, the single adult, the homeless, the broken and searching, the timid and shy?

Putting yourself in their shoes is powerful. Imagine yourself standing in the church parking lot feeling excluded or fearing you will be excluded. Imagine feeling a yearning for love and belonging yet being too paralyzed by fear to go in the building. Imagine Jesus standing there with you, watching and weeping over the situation.

I don't think this is what God dreamed of for His church or His people. Who are we to deny love or friendship to someone who seeks it? Moreover, what can we do to make people feel the freedom to walk into our churches? It might help us to keep in mind that Jesus' ministry was one of inclusion, and in fact, He criticized the church of His day more than He ever did the people outside it. That is because He expects us to know better and rightfully holds us accountable for our disobedience.

> "So if you know of an opportunity to do the right thing today, yet you refrain from doing it, you're guilty of sin" (James 4:7 TPT).

Community of Friends

"Two are better than one, because they have a good return for their labor: If either of them falls down, one can help the other up. But pity anyone who falls and has no one to help them up" (Ecclesiastes 4:9-10 NIV).

After work yesterday, I spent some much-needed time with my best friend in celebration of her birthday. She and I have been best friends for seventeen years. I never had a best friend growing up, and thus I cherish her friendship so much.

We first met at church and soon discovered that we had several things in common. Our children were born on the same day, four years apart; we were married the same year; and both of us were English majors in college. Our children went to private school together, and eventually, they were also homeschooled and attended public school as well. We also share many similar viewpoints and experiences.

Although we have these similarities, we also have major differences. I have lived apart from family and have been a widow for many years; she grew up locally and still has her family close by her, and her husband is still alive. She lifts weights and runs; I swim and do yoga. I prefer to sit at home and write or watch a movie, and she'd rather read a book or climb a mountain. She is goal-oriented and self-motivating, and I tend to take each day as it comes.

In combination, we make each other stronger. We vent to each other, encourage one another, and pray for each other all the time. We trust and love each other as sisters making our way in the world.

My friend and I are a type of supportive community, but we are just two of the members of our church family. Like most churches, we call our church congregation a family because, like a family, we support each other, we defend each other, and sometimes we quarrel with each other. However, as a body of believers united in the love of Christ, our church and all churches should strive to be families who honor Him. We should, furthermore, seek to expand our horizons, warmly welcoming others into God's family. By doing such, we might find a forever friend.

> "Let the peace of Christ rule in your hearts, since as members of one body you were called to peace. And be thankful. Let the message of Christ dwell among you richly as you teach and admonish one another with all wisdom through psalms, hymns, and songs from the Spirit, singing to God with gratitude in your hearts" (Colossians 3:15-16 NIV).

Worship Styles

"Sing to the Lord, for he has done glorious things; let this be known to all the world" (Isaiah 12:5 NIV).

Whenever I go visit my family in Ohio, I enjoy visiting their church. They have always welcomed me as one of their own even though I live two states away. I count it a blessing to be a part of their fellowship.

Because there is a large deaf community in this church, a sign-language interpreter is always present on stage for the service. I didn't understand the need for an interpreter during the song service when the words were projected on the screen until I watched the interpreter sign to the songs. I noticed that he signed each song with movements of praise and reverence and stretched the words out according to the melody. The deaf in the audience read his emotions, facial expressions, and the speed and force of his hand movements to feel the spirit of the song. The spirit combines the music, singing, and sign language to create a beautiful and moving rhapsody of worship.

I had a similar experience back home when I watched a four-year-old dance in the aisles of our church sanctuary during a song service one day. She couldn't read the lyrics to sing along, so she worshipped in her own way by swaying and twirling to the music. While some in our church may have found her dance distracting, I found it to be a sweet and tender addition to my worship experience.

I am sure these worship experiences pale in comparison to what God sees and hears. He must enjoy the sounds and sights of all of us, His children, praising Him for who He is in our lives. I imagine that the languages and the styles must combine into something lovely, and it must bless His heart to receive our love.

> "My lips brim praises like fountains. I bless you every time I take a breath; My arms wave like banners of praise to you" (Psalm 63:3b-4 MSG).

Dedication of the Temple

> "Then the temple of the Lord was filled with the cloud, and the priests could not perform their service because of the cloud, for the glory of the Lord filled the temple of God" (2 Chronicles 5:13b-14 NIV).

I was privileged to participate in the centennial anniversary of the church where I worship. Since we were expecting former members, pastors, and guests to join us for the festivities, we wanted the church to look its best. Therefore, we held an extensive workday the day before the event, and all those who were available and willing spent the day cleaning and painting the facilities. When I went in later that evening to train tour guides, I was astounded at the beauty of our church. Excitement was growing as we worked together to get everything ready.

As thrilling as it was for us, I couldn't help wondering what it was like to be present at the dedication service of God's temple built under the direction of King Solomon. Until then, God had moved among His people in a portable tabernacle. Finally, the people were able to worship in a temple built on the land He had promised them. I can only imagine the fresh construction smell of newly harvested cedar wood, the glitter of the gold and silver ornaments, and the brightness of the new, crisp priestly garments. The temple must have been beautiful when completed, but I bet it paled in comparison to how awesome it looked filled with the cloud of God's glory.

This train of thought made me wonder: shouldn't we come to church with expectation every Sunday? Shouldn't we arrive with excitement and anticipation of what is going to happen in God's house that day? Are we attending church on auto-pilot and thus never experiencing God in our worship?

Often when that happens, we blame the church. However, God doesn't dwell in the building, the worship, or its programs; rather, He dwells in the individual hearts of its people. Therefore, if we want God to inhabit our worship, we have to prepare our hearts for His presence. In so doing, we will be ready to experience His Spirit when we meet together in worship.

> "After they prayed, the place where they were meeting was shaken. And they were all filled with the Holy Spirit and spoke the word of God boldly. All the believers were one in heart and mind" (Acts 4:31-32a NIV).

Cuddles or Claws?

"As she stood behind [Jesus] at his feet weeping, she began to wet his feet with her tears. Then she wiped them with her hair, kissed them and poured perfume on them. When the Pharisee who had invited him saw this, he said to himself, 'If this man were a prophet, he would know who is touching him and what kind of woman she is—that she is a sinner'" (Luke 7:38-39 NIV).

When my daughter left for graduate school, she left me home with our two cats: an older one and a one-year-old kitten. I guess she officially made me a "cat lady." With her gone, the cats found themselves alone most of the day while I worked. Therefore, they developed a daily routine to try to keep me home. When I sat on my bed to put on my socks, the kitten, who has an abundance of energy, pounced up next to me with his claws out, wanting to play. The older cat laid belly-up on top of my feet, tempting me to pet him. He knew I had a weakness for a cat's soft, white, furry belly. I would have loved to stay home with them, but I must admit I would much rather stay to cuddle with the older cat than be pounced, scratched, and bitten by the younger one.

I imagine Jesus felt that way in this scene from Luke. He had prickly Pharisees beside Him, waiting for another opportunity to pounce on Him. At His feet was a broken woman who had given all she had in worship and adoration for Him. I imagine Jesus felt love, grace, and mercy for the woman, but at the same time, He felt sadness for the Pharisee who thought her worshipful actions foolish.

I, like many Christians, want to be the type of person who trusts Jesus enough to lay everything down at His feet in worship and surrender. However, sadly, that is not always the case. Sometimes I find myself fighting internally to hold back from Him.

We are blessed that Jesus loves us and forgives us mercifully. This powerful love kept Him on the cross where He endured excruciating pain at our hands. His precious body was struck with spikes and a spear, and He took all these blows to defeat death and restore our relationship with Him. For that alone, He is most deserving of all the love we have for Him, and we should willingly pour everything we have at His feet in worship.

> "Ascribe to the Lord the glory due his name; bring an offering and come before him. Worship the Lord in the splendor of his holiness" (1 Chronicles 16:29 NIV).

Basking in the Son

> "When Jesus spoke again to the people, he said, 'I am the light of the world. Whoever follows me will never walk in darkness, but will have the light of life'" (John 8:12 NIV).

Have you ever noticed how animals, both wild and domestic, will seek a sunbeam to lie down in? I've definitely seen this tendency in my cats. They have one particular spot on the floor in front of my sliding glass door where they love to bask in the sun. They work themselves between two layers of curtains and the window to get as close to the sun as they possibly can. Then they stretch out for a long day of sleeping. I love to pick them up after they've been there for a while so I can feel their warm fur against my skin.

Humans also need sunshine, and some of us annually trek out to the beach in order to be near it. Not only is the sunshine warm and cozy, it is also good for us. In fact, doctors recommend we get out in the sun a few minutes each day because the sun has many health benefits. It helps us produce Vitamin D, which strengthens our bones. It wards off seasonal depression and gives us energy. It also may have pain-relieving and healing qualities as well.

As Christians, we also have to bask in the light of the Son each day. Spending time in God's presence through prayer, Bible reading, and worship recharges our souls and renews our minds. This connection with God gives us strength and energy for each day.

God also fills us up with His light so that we can shine it on others who don't yet even realize their need for it. We hope this will pique their interest and lead to their salvation. We cannot be used in this way, however, until we take time to properly soak up God's Sonlight.

> "You, Lord, are my lamp; the Lord turns my darkness into light. With your help I can advance against a troop; with my God I can scale a wall" (2 Samuel 22:29-30 NIV).

Spring Has Sprung!

> "The Lord God took the man and put him in the Garden of Eden to work it and take care of it" (Genesis 2:15 NIV).

Each day as I leave my house, I glance out over my yard to see if anything needs to be done. In the short walk from my house to my car, the amount of work I see can overwhelm me. Springtime is the worst because everything is growing and seeding, and yard work is always needed. My grass and bushes grow quickly, and dandelion stems and maple seeds always seem prolific. The sight can be discouraging.

One day as I looked over the new crop of dandelion stems and maple seeds, I thought to myself, "Spring, you are so messy." Then I looked up and saw my azalea bushes in full bloom. I was awestruck by their beauty; they looked the best they've looked in years. I forgot about the madness around me as I gazed upon their pink and white blooms.

The Holy Spirit took this opportunity to teach me about potential. While I cherish the azalea bushes while they are blooming, I don't the rest of the year. However, since I look forward to that day, I don't cut them down during the other eleven months when they are not so pretty.

God then drew my attention to the maple seeds. Though they are not as beautiful as the flowers and they are inconvenient and messy, they also have potential to grow into large, leafy maple trees.

Suddenly, I could understand how God looks at us. He doesn't see us as billions of pieces of trash cluttering His world. He sees each of us as His beautiful children with potential for bright futures. We may not always be blooming, but we are still valuable. We are His workmanship, the branches holding His vine. With God's pruning and watering, we will grow to be strong and healthy testimonies, spreading seeds of the gospel to many others around us.

> "But blessed is the one who trusts in the Lord, whose confidence is in him. They will be like a tree planted by the water that sends out its roots by the stream. It does not fear when heat comes; its leaves are always green. It has no worries in a year of drought and never fails to bear fruit" (Jeremiah 17:7-8 NIV).

Faith Is Power

> "He replied, 'Because you have so little faith. Truly I tell you, if you have faith as small as a mustard seed, you can say to this mountain, "Move from here to there," and it will move. Nothing will be impossible for you'" (Matthew 17:20 NIV).

When I was a little girl, I used to enjoy playing with the costume jewelry in my mom's jewelry box. One particular necklace captivated my attention every time: a gold chain with a tiny little tube on it which encased several tiny yellow seeds. When I asked my mom about it, she explained that the seeds were mustard seeds, and the charm referenced Matthew 17:20, serving as a reminder to have faith.

Faith is an act of surrender. It is yielding our will even if we don't know the future. It is the act of love and trust which God requires to do mighty things in our lives.

An excellent example of faith is the story of the little boy and his lunch, found in all four gospels. Though there were multitudes of hungry people, this boy offered up his lunch to Jesus, showing Jesus that he trusted Him to use it in some helpful way. Jesus took that boy's lunch, blessed it, and used it to feed thousands of people with many baskets left over. Alone, the boy could not satisfy the hunger of the multitudes, but with God's power, he did.

This story shows that when we put our faith in God, we become empowered and useful to Him. He takes our grains of faith, even ones as small as mustard seeds or a little boy's lunch, and uses them in a mighty way. We will be amazed at all He can accomplish with our faithful hearts.

> "Now all glory to God, who is able, through his mighty power at work within us, to accomplish infinitely more than we might ask or think" (Ephesians 3:20 NLT).

Getting the Spot Out

> "For as high as the heavens are above the earth, so great is his love for those who fear him; as far as the east is from the west, so far has he removed our transgressions from us" (Psalm 103:11-12 NIV).

I used to have a pretty, white throw blanket which was given to me and my husband at our wedding. One day, when my daughter was about ten, we discovered something had been spilled on it, leaving a huge, dark stain. My daughter, recognizing the significance of the blanket, asked if she could try to clean it up, and I gave her my consent. She soaked it in pure bleach for a long time before washing it. When the blanket came out of the washer, we were both shocked to see that it was in two pieces. We now had a throw blanket with a perfectly round hole in it and a tiny round blanket which was still stained. We both laughed at the fact that she had succeeded in removing the spot completely from the blanket! We no longer have the throw, but I kept the little spot as a fun reminder.

Just as the stain was removed from the throw, so does God remove our transgressions from us if we earnestly seek His forgiveness. He casts our sins far from us, and He does not remember them anymore. His forgiveness enables us to enjoy a restored relationship with Him because our sin no longer separates us from Him. Though we may still be left with consequences of our sin, our Father sees our hearts as whole again.

> "Come, let's talk this over, says the Lord; no matter how deep the stain of your sins, I can take it out and make you as clean as freshly fallen snow. Even if you are stained as red as crimson, I can make you white as wool!" (Isaiah 1:18 TLB).

Relationships Matter

> "But Jesus said, 'Let the little children come to me and do not hinder them, for to such belongs the kingdom of heaven'" (Matthew 19:14 ESV).

It is Vacation Bible School time again! The time when the Children's Pastor is flustered and can no longer fit in his own office. The time when volunteers scurry to finish last minute preparations.

Despite being a child who was taken to church every time the doors were opened, I really looked forward to VBS each year. It was in the morning in those days, and there were no elaborate themes. We marched in the sanctuary by school grade to "Onward Christian

Soldiers," pledged to the flags and the Bible, and joyfully sang some Sunday School songs. After the pastor or director welcomed us, we were dismissed to our classrooms.

Besides snack-time and crafts, there were two specific reasons why I loved VBS. I loved being allowed to go into a different room, especially one used by adults on Sunday. I also loved having new teachers whom I didn't really know. I formed many life-changing, mentoring relationships in these VBS classrooms.

Today's VBS is usually thematic, often engaging children through multimedia in an effort to attract and excite them. We have to stay relevant, and this type of VBS reflects the media-driven world in which we live. However, one aspect remains important and cannot be done through a video screen, and that is the formation of relationships. Jesus met people where they were in His ministry, and He is our example to follow. He wants all children who come through the church doors to leave knowing they have a caring friend at church and are deeply loved by God.

> "He put a child in the middle of the room. Then, cradling the little one in his arms, he said, 'Whoever embraces one of these children as I do embraces me, and far more than me—God who sent me'" (Mark 9:36-37 MSG).

Going Back to School

> "Then he said, 'I tell you the truth, unless you turn from your sins and become like little children, you will never get into the Kingdom of Heaven'" (Matthew 18:3 NLT).

I had the opportunity to visit a local elementary school recently with some of my friends, one of whom is a former student of this school. Now, she is a teacher at another local elementary school.

As we walked through the school, I could see by the look on her face that she was remembering her days there as a child. Only now, she was looking at it as an adult with teacher's eyes. She could not contain her surprise at how small everything seemed to be in comparison to how big she had seen it as a child. It was clear that the school building seemed pretty much the same, but her perspective was definitely different.

Adults and children often see things differently. To a small child, the world seems huge; as an adult, the same world can seem very small. Children look at the world through innocent eyes, and adults usually look at the world with cautious, protective eyes.

Jesus told us that we are to come to Him in the same way small, innocent children do, approaching Him innocently with love, complete trust, and boldness. We are to feel safe in yielding our care and protection into His hands. We are to walk beside Him as a son or daughter while listening to His wise instruction. We are to show Him respect and obedience.

While we may see God differently throughout our lifetime, God looks at us the same our whole lives. We are His beloved children. We always have been, and we always will be.

"I will instruct you and teach you in the way you should go; I will counsel you with my loving eye on you" (Psalm 32:8 NIV).

Treasure, Not Trash

"Though my father and mother forsake me, the Lord will receive me" (Psalm 27:10 NIV).

When my daughter worked with foster children, my eyes were opened to the constant heartbreak of children in the system. While she never shared specifics with me, she shared facts that were common to most foster kids. These facts were sometimes hard to hear, but they made me sensitive to the complicated lives of foster children, their families, and foster care parents.

I can only imagine what it is like as a small child to have a stranger suddenly appear at their home, pack up all their belongings in a trash bag, and then take them to live with other strangers in their home. Most of the time the children are better off, but that doesn't mean they understand. Just think about it: they see the trash taken away by strangers and it never comes back, and now they are being carried off just like the trash.

To combat this, groups seek to minimize or eliminate the "trash bag trauma" by collecting luggage and making quilted bags to use when moving children from their home or foster home. While seemingly insignificant, these bags make the children feel cared for and make the transition a little better. The situation does not seem as permanent or destructive as being thrown out like the garbage.

This idea made me think of Jesus' ministry. He truly valued people, considering no one a lost cause or a piece of trash. He intentionally reached out to those who were sick or outcast. He even went the extra mile and physically laid His tender hands upon the diseased and sought out known thieves, prostitutes, and adulterers. Jesus made it clear that everyone was important and loved, even His enemies. He loved people even when they refused to receive His unconditional love. Jesus' love for all of us was the very heart of His message, a message that He asks us to share with the world.

> "'Now which of these three would you say was a neighbor to the man who was attacked by bandits?' Jesus asked. The man replied, 'The one who showed him mercy.' Then Jesus said, 'Yes, now go and do the same'" (Luke 10: 36-37 NLT).

Embracing the Calling

〰️

> "But the Lord said to Samuel, 'Do not consider his appearance or his height, for I have rejected him. The Lord does not look at the things people look at. People look at the outward appearance, but the Lord looks at the heart'" (1 Samuel 16:7 NIV).

God told Samuel to anoint David as king of His people even though he was a young shepherd boy. David's father and his brothers didn't see him as king material. In fact, they left him in the field shepherding the flock when Samuel asked to see all the sons. God wanted David, however, and He had Samuel summon him in from the fields.

David is historically known as an emotional, thoughtful, and intelligent person who may have been prone to depression, as evidenced by some of his psalms. So I imagine David felt rejected when he realized he was the only one left in the fields guarding his family's sheep when Samuel came for a visit. As the youngest of many sons, this disappointment was probably just one of many. He had probably been overlooked often for being "too young" or "too small." He must have been shocked to have been brought to Samuel and anointed as God's choice as the next king.

Even though David was called and anointed, he still had to choose to embrace the calling and trust God's process if he wanted to achieve it. It was not an easy process either; he had to fight for his kingdom. That same choice is ours every day. If we want to live out our faith and find our purpose, we have to partner with God and follow His leadership. On our own, we can achieve good things, but with God's assistance we can do greater things.

> "Not that I have already obtained all this, or have already arrived at my goal, but I press on to take hold of that for which Christ Jesus took hold of me" (Philippians 3:12 NIV).

Waiting for God

"So Samuel took the horn of oil and anointed him in the presence of his brothers, and from that day on the Spirit of the Lord came powerfully upon David. Samuel then went to Ramah" (1 Samuel 16:13 NIV).

Biblical scholars estimate that David was between ten and fifteen years old when Samuel anointed him as king. He didn't, however, become king of Judah until around fifteen years later, and then he became king of Israel after another seven years. Therefore, David's anointing was the beginning of a long, arduous twenty-plus-year journey toward becoming king of Israel.

God had several reasons for making David wait. First, Saul was already serving as king when David was anointed, and Saul was angry about God wanting to replace him. Secondly, as pointed out earlier, David was young, and he needed time to grow and mature. Thirdly, David needed to grow spiritually, learning to trust and rely on God and to seek His will before making decisions for the people. Though it was a long wait, it was certainly needed and was time well-spent preparing David to reign over God's chosen people.

Waiting is not easy, especially when we don't know why. We easily get tired and impatient, and we struggle to stay hopeful and optimistic. Despite these feelings, it is helpful to remember that God is still working. He is getting us ready, working things out, and waiting for the right time. He has a real purpose for our wait, and hopefully we will understand the reason when it is over. Waiting is tough, but we will surely benefit if we do not give up.

"We also have joy with our troubles, because we know that these troubles produce patience. And patience produces character, and character produces hope" (Romans 5:3-4 NCV).

Putting on the Right Armor

♥

"Stand firm then, with the belt of truth buckled around your waist, with the breastplate of righteousness in place, and with your feet fitted with the readiness that comes from the gospel of peace. In addition to all this, take up the shield of faith, with which you can extinguish all the flaming arrows of the evil one. Take the helmet of salvation and the sword of the Spirit, which is the word of God" (Ephesians 6:14-17 NIV).

As I read this passage about spiritual armor, God brought to my mind the story of David and Goliath (1 Samuel 17). In this story, David, who was probably in his mid-teens, volunteered to fight a Philistine giant who had intimidated Israel's army for days. David pled with King Saul to let him fight the giant, and Saul agreed but asked David to wear his own coat of armor as protection. However, as David tried walking around in it, he decided to take it off because he was not used to it. He felt it was of no help to him because he had not previously trained in it; therefore, his life would have been more at risk with the armor than without it. David goes on to stand up against the giant in the name of the Lord, defeating him with a stone, a sling shot, and the giant's own sword.

This story is an excellent illustration of the importance of choosing the correct armor. Our adversary, like Goliath, wants nothing more than to curse our God, ruin our testimony, and stop the momentum and effectiveness of God's power in our lives. We can't fight these spiritual battles using fleshly armor and weapons.

We play into our enemy's evil plan when we, like the Israelites, choose to live in fear. Fear separates us from God and keeps us stuck and defeated. Every time we give in to fear, we give our adversary the victory. David clothed himself in faith and hope, choosing to rely on God's power to defeat the giant. This same spiritual armor is ours for the asking, and it is every bit as effective and powerful now as it was then.

"For our struggle is not against flesh and blood, but against the rulers, against the authorities, against the powers of this dark world and against the spiritual forces of evil in the heavenly realms. Therefore put on the full armor of God, so that when the day of evil comes, you may be able to stand your ground, and after you have done everything, to stand" (Ephesians 6:12-13 NIV).

Help for the Dried-Up Soul

"My soul faints with longing for your salvation, but I have put my hope in your word. My eyes fail, looking for your promise; I say, 'When will you comfort me?' Though I am like a wineskin in the smoke, I do not forget your decrees" (Psalm 119:81-83 NIV).

As I read this passage, my curiosity piqued. The phrase "like a wineskin in the smoke" was something I never noticed before, and I didn't know what it meant. So I decided to research it.

In my investigation, I discovered that a wineskin was a drinking container made from animal hide. The Israelites would hang the skin over the heat of the fire to dry it out so it could hold liquid. Wineskins were also hung over the fire in tents to absorb the smoke and keep it from filling up the tent. If a wineskin was hung over the fire for an extended period, it became dried out and misshapen, and the smoke would change the taste of the wine.

From this verse, we can see that David was comparing himself to a dried out, useless, empty, misshapen, smoky animal hide. He was feeling low and disconnected from God. Despite his feelings, however, he held on to faith and hope, still trusting God to keep His promises.

Like David, we can sometimes feel abandoned and empty of God's

Spirit when we are going through struggles and tough times. I know I felt that way when I was struggling with depression. Looking back on those days now, however, I can see how my feelings misled me. God had not left me; He was with me the entire time, leading me out of my depression. He was my stronghold in the storm and my guide through the darkness. I learned the truth of His promise to never leave us or forsake us (Hebrews 13:5). It's not about feelings; it's about faith.

> "God . . . turned the curse into a blessing for you, because the Lord your God loves you" (Deuteronomy 23:5b NIV).

Always Have Hope

> "Do not be far from me, my God; come quickly, God, to help me. May my accusers perish in shame; may those who want to harm me be covered with scorn and disgrace. As for me, I will always have hope; I will praise you more and more" (Psalm 71:12-14 NIV).

As I read this, I was particularly struck by verse 14. I love that David said, "I will *always* have hope." After listing all the trouble his enemies were giving him, he declared with triumphal praise that he would always put his hope in God. God had proven Himself trustworthy, so David felt secure putting his faith in Him.

When we rely on God, we can rest assured that we are putting our hope in someone who will never let us down or be taken away from us. This hope is powerful, so powerful that it forces the devil to flee (James 4:7). He cannot compete with that kind of strength, so knowing he can't win, he runs away.

Hope in God is a powerful and passionate gift of the Spirit. It uplifts our souls, submits our wills to God's, and defeats the adversary. The Holy Spirit further honors our faith by giving us peace. We can't explain it or understand it, but we can take it as proof that God acknowledges our faith in Him.

> "I pray that God, the source of hope, will fill you completely with joy and peace because you trust in him. Then you will overflow with confident hope through the power of the Holy Spirit" (Romans 15:13 NLT).

While Our Enemies Watch

> "You prepare a table before me in the presence of my enemies. You anoint my head with oil; my cup overflows" (Psalm 23:5 NIV).

The 23rd psalm is a chapter that many people have memorized. It is a good psalm to read as a reminder of God's presence and care during times of uncertainty. Verse five is a powerful little gem in the midst of this beautiful psalm.

In this verse, David says that God prepares a table *in front* of his enemies. Since the enemies are watching, we know they are still alive. So God is celebrating David's victory before the battle is even won.

This verse also speaks of God's provision. In the midst of our troubling circumstances, God gives us what we need. He gives us strength when we are weak, truth when faced with lies, hope when we are grieving, encouragement when we are depressed, security when we feel vulnerable. He offers what we need when we need it.

Not only is God working in our lives, but He is also working in the lives of our enemies who are watching. God's strength is vividly on display when we are at our weakest. Our faith in God brings our enemies face-to-face with a real and powerful God as He works on our behalf.

Whatever enemy we face, God can help us overcome. Even death is no match for Him, for through our death, we are given a brand new life.

"I have told you these things, so that in me you may have peace. In this world you will have trouble. But take heart! I have overcome the world" (John 16:33 NIV).

Sleeping in Peace

💕

"A furious squall came up, and the waves broke over the boat, so that it was nearly swamped. Jesus was in the stern, sleeping on a cushion. The disciples woke him and said to him, 'Teacher, don't you care if we drown?'" (Mark 4:37-38 NIV).

When my nephew was a little over a month old, we took him to watch the July 4th fireworks. By the time we got there, he had fallen sleep in his car seat, and to our surprise, he slept soundly through the entire show. He was sleeping so hard that he didn't even flinch when the loud booms blasted. We were all amazed. I thought to myself that it must be awesome to blissfully sleep that soundly.

My nephew's ability to sleep during fireworks reminded me of Jesus sleeping in the boat as it was tossed in the sea during a storm. The disciples, some of whom were seasoned fishermen, were genuinely afraid. They decided to wake Jesus to tell Him they were about to die. Jesus didn't panic, but instead He calmly spoke to the wind and quieted the storm, creating a great calm both within His disciples and outside the boat. The disciples were amazed by Jesus' power.

My nephew could sleep because his mind was clear and he felt secure in his family's care. Jesus rested the same way by placing Himself in His Father's care. We have access to the Father's watchful care too when we place our faith, hope, and trust in Him. He will honor this act by giving us a peaceful calm which we cannot generate on our own, our assurance that He is there and working on our behalf.

"You keep him in perfect peace whose mind is stayed on you, because he trusts in you" (Isaiah 26:3 ESV).

Timely Priorities

"In vain you rise early and stay up late, toiling for food to eat—for he grants sleep to those he loves" (Psalm 127:2 NIV).

My women's Bible study group has been discussing God's view of resting. At the beginning of the study, many of the ladies in the group, most of whom have young children and teenagers, brought up the fact that there is no room in their schedules for rest. Many said they get up at the crack of dawn to exercise, and they are usually one of the last of their household to go to sleep at night because they are taking care of their families.

Apparently, we took the idea to heart because at our last meeting, we were stunned to discover that most of us hadn't done the chapter in our study guide because we were resting. We no longer cared if we completed everything on our to-do lists because we were making time for ourselves. Unfortunately, we went too far, for spending time with God had not been a priority that week.

The truth is we all have the same amount of time in a day, and it is our choice as to what we do with it. The item, task, or person that is most important to us will be found on the top of our daily priority list. Unfortunately, if we don't make spending time with God a top priority, there is a good chance it may not even make it into our day.

Jesus, our example, spent His mornings communing with the Father, and I imagine that their dialogue continued throughout the day. He heavily leaned on His Father for guidance, always following His Father's leadership. He watched for His Father to work, and He joined Him in this work (John 5:19) because it was of utmost importance to Him.

I wonder what our lives would look like if we did the same. What if we spent the mornings with Him and kept the dialogue open all day? What if we watched for God's work and listened for His voice throughout our day? I venture to guess that our relationship with Him would be stronger and our lives more meaningful than we could ever imagine.

> "I rise before dawn and cry for help; I have put my hope in your word. My eyes stay open through the watches of the night, that I may meditate on your promises" (Psalm 119:147-148 NIV).

Rest from Our Labors

> "Come to me, all you who are weary and burdened, and I will give you rest. Take my yoke upon you and learn from me, for I am gentle and humble in heart, and you will find rest for your souls. For my yoke is easy and my burden is light" (Matthew 11:28-30 NIV).

This verse has been one of my favorites, and I've had it memorized for a long time. It is a comforting verse because it promises peace and rest. As I studied in order to teach it recently though, God gave me brand new insight.

The verse speaks to those who "labor and are heavy laden." I have always grouped those two terms together as a way to describe working really, really hard. I learned, however, that these are two distinct terms: labor denotes work we put upon ourselves while heavy laden refers to work that is placed upon us by someone else.

So in thinking about these words, I wondered how often we try to serve on our own without God's help and how often we take on projects that we should not be doing at all. It is easy to take on too much when we are willing to serve. Unfortunately, when we do, we frequently find ourselves struggling to get started, not doing a good job when we do get started, and feeling exhausted from trying. This state is definitely not easy on the body or peaceful for the soul.

Our burden will ease when we are doing what God calls us to do. He will reveal the best path for us if we ask Him. Then when we follow through in faith, we will find ourselves joyfully serving with a passion and purpose. Our bodies and souls will be energized as we do amazing works in the power of God.

> "He gives power to the faint, and to him who has no might he increases strength" (Isaiah 40:29 ESV).

An Easy Yoke

> "Come to me, all you who are weary and burdened, and I will give you rest. Take my yoke upon you and learn from me, for I am gentle and humble in heart, and you will find rest for your souls. For my yoke is easy and my burden is light" (Matthew 11:28-30 NIV).

As I continued my study of Matthew 11:28-30, I then focused on the yoke Jesus mentions. A yoke is a wooden piece of farm equipment which goes around the necks of oxen to couple them together for plowing. When a young or new ox is in training, the farmer will often partner it with a more experienced animal. The experienced ox then leads and trains the other to follow the farmer's directions as they work the plow for him.

I have always thought the oxen referred to us in this story with Jesus as the farmer. However, after reading this analogy, it seems that we are yoked beside Jesus. He is the experienced leader in the relationship who is guiding while pulling beside us. In this way, he helps us carry our burdens.

The passage tells us that His yoke is easy and His leadership gentle and lowly, which is important. For if a headstrong, ill-mannered ox is yoked to a younger one, there would be a lot of pulling on the yoke, causing physical harm to the animals' necks. Not only that, but this friction makes it tough for the farmer to get any plowing done. This verse tells us that Jesus leads with gentle guidance and encouragement, working at a pace we are able to follow. His yoke is helpful and not harmful to us.

Our task in this yoked relationship is to learn to follow His leadership. He is our resource for finding the best path, the easiest pace, and the most beneficial practices in carrying our burdens. Thus, if we follow His leadership, our load will lighten, our faith and trust in Him will strengthen, and we will find rest for our weary souls.

> "Don't panic. I'm with you. There's no need to fear for I'm your God. I'll give you strength. I'll help you. I'll hold you steady, keep a firm grip on you" (Isaiah 41:10 MSG).

Being Perfect

"Be perfect, therefore, as your heavenly Father is perfect" (Matthew 5:48 NIV).

When my Bible study group came across this verse, we were all puzzled by it. I especially perked up because I am a recovering perfectionist. I didn't understand why Jesus would tell us to be something we could never achieve.

This verse is at the end of Matthew chapter five, which is the first chapter of the Sermon on the Mount. This chapter contains the Beatitudes and encouragements to follow God's laws not only in our actions but also in our hearts. In context, this verse seems to sum up the chapter and speaks of growing in spiritual maturity and becoming Christlike.

I love the way the CEV version puts the verse: "But you must always act like your Father in heaven." It is a modern day "What would Jesus do?" We are to strive to have the mind of Christ as He is our example of how our Father wants us to act. The Father wants the world to know Him through us, a people full of grace, forgiveness, kindness, and most importantly love. For God indeed is love, and the world desperately needs to be shown love.

"My command is this: Love each other as I have loved you" (John 15:12 NIV).

You Can't Go Home Again

♥

"When his time of service was completed, he returned home" (Luke 1:23 NIV).

Recently when I was in Ohio, I decided to stop by the house where I grew up. I hadn't seen it in a while, and I just wanted to lay my eyes on it again. So I drove over there and parked across the street to take a picture.

As I looked at the house, I, of course, grew nostalgic thinking about when I lived there. I remembered the fun we had when my grandparents, aunt, uncle, mom, sister, and I all lived there together. I remembered how we used to play board and card games and bake Christmas cookies together. I remembered raking leaves, planting the garden, hanging out the wash, and swimming in our small above-ground pool. I remembered walking up and down the alleys to the local store to pick up items for the family and to exchange soda bottles to buy chips or ice cream. The list of memories could go on and on.

Putting the past aside and looking at the house in the present, I noticed that it resembled every other house in the neighborhood built nearly a hundred years ago. There was nothing special about it that would draw someone's attention to it. It was just a house that another family now lived in, and as many times as I have walked in that door without knocking, I was no longer welcome to do so. What had made it my home was my family, and without my family, it was just a house.

Spiritually speaking, I thought about how that one day this earth and my body will no longer be my home. My past and everything I have gained and worked hard for in this world will stay behind me when I walk into my new heavenly home. The memory of me and the influence that I have had on those who continue living will be all that remains of me on this planet, and even that may only last a couple more generations.

Our heavenly home, on the other hand, will be eternal. We will be surrounded with loved ones who have gone on before us, and once again, our homes will be blessed with family. Best of all though, we will be able to physically be in the presence of God. Can you imagine having tea with Jesus? You never know: it may be one of the perks of living in the Kingdom of God.

> "For we know that if the tent that is our earthly home is destroyed, we have a building from God, a house not made with hands, eternal in the heavens" (2 Corinthians 5:1 ESV).

Discovering Our Heritage

"One generation commends your works to another; they tell of your mighty acts" (Psalm 145:4 NIV).

One evening my daughter came in to the living room carrying my wedding album and my high school scrapbook. She sat down on the couch and started flipping through the books. The more she looked, the more questions she asked. Then suddenly, she became quiet and began to cry. She finally explained to me that the tears came from reading a handwritten Valentine's Day poem her dad had written to me. She said she had been longing to read one of our love letters and also to see her dad's handwriting. Since her dad had passed away when she was young, she had never seen his writing before or heard anything about our relationship from him. This letter so moved her because it was both of these in the same document, profoundly touching her heart.

She explained to me as we talked late into the night that she was searching for her identity and wanted to know more about the history of us, her parents. All she knew of our relationship was what she had seen in pictures and heard from me and others. The handwritten expression of her dad's love shared his side of our story with her and gave her a glimpse into his heart, making him feel real to her again.

In the same way, if we want to know more about our Heavenly Father and our spiritual history, we have to read the Bible. In it, we find the history of humanity, which is a long love story between our Creator and His creation, chronicling the lengths Jesus went through to free us from the deadly consequences of sin. It shares advice and lists God's expectations and guidelines for living. It contains the writing of many authors who wrote in song, poetry, narrative, and prophecy. It is so much more than a religious primer: it is the living and breathing Word of God.

> "All Scripture is God-breathed and is useful for teaching, rebuking, correcting and training in righteousness, so that the servant of God may be thoroughly equipped for every good work" (2 Timothy 3:16-17 NIV).

Going to the Fair with Grandpa

♡

"Grandchildren are the crown of aged men, And the glory of children is their fathers [who live godly lives]" (Proverbs 17:6 AMP).

Most summers when I was little, I would stay a week with my paternal grandparents when the local county fair was going on. We would spend our evenings at the fair together doing something fun, such as watching my aunt and uncle participate in the demolition derby. At the end of the week, I would usually come home with a bag full of sugar waffles and a "free" goldfish I had won by landing a ping-pong ball in its bowl.

My most favorite memories of the fair revolve around my grandpa. He and I would go to the tractor pulls together every year. I was too young to understand them, and the loud engine noise scared me, but I loved to go because my grandpa loved watching them with me. We would also enjoy an annual "date" to the church tent for hot roast beef sandwiches. If I were lucky, we would make a couple of visits to this tent.

I had no doubt that my grandpa loved me. I could see it his actions and in the way his eyes twinkled as he escorted me around the fair introducing me to his friends. I stayed on my best behavior because I wanted to make him happy.

My grandpa modeled for me how a relationship with God should work. We should always know we are loved by Him. Thus, we should want to please Him with our obedience and devotion in order to earn His smile of pride and approval. We should make time to be with Him because we enjoy being together. Our desire and hope should be that when we finally stand before God in our new bodies, we will be able to see a twinkle of pride in his eyes as he says to us, "Well done, my good and faithful child."

"There's a crown of righteousness waiting in heaven for me, and I know that my Lord will reward me on his day of righteous judgment. And this crown is not only waiting for me, but for all who love and long for his unveiling (2 Timothy 4:7-8 TPT).

Looking for Heroes

"One generation commends your works to another; they tell of your mighty acts" (Psalm 145:4 NIV).

Recently, I heard a youth pastor give a report from a survey he had taken of his youth group. One of the questions he asked the students was to name three of their heroes and give an explanation as to why they were their heroes. Most of the students gave the names of their parents, grandparents, pastors, and youth pastors. One student, however, gave a unique answer which I thought profound. He said Batman was his hero because he proved that you don't have to have superpowers to be a hero.

What this student said is true: you don't have to have superpowers to be a hero. In fact, the survey itself proved that to be true. Most of the heroes mentioned by the youth group were ordinary people just living their lives. The students said they chose these people as their heroes because the person spent time with them, showed them how to forgive by forgiving, worked hard, loved unconditionally, and/or overcame great obstacles.

A follow-up question the youth pastor asked was how did the students best learn from their heroes. Almost all of the students replied that it was by example—not anything these heroes said but what they showed the students through their lives. I venture to guess that most of these heroes didn't even know they were being watched by the students.

My takeaway from this report was that children of all ages need good role models. They are watching us, adults, whether we realize it or not. Therefore, we should be careful of what we say, what decisions we make, and how we react to life. The best way for us to do this is to follow Jesus, our own hero. He will give us the power we need to lead others to Him.

"Always set an example by doing good things. When you teach, be an example of moral purity and dignity. Speak an accurate message that cannot be condemned. Then those who oppose us will be ashamed because they cannot say anything bad about us" (Titus 2:7-8 GW).

Serving with Joy

♡

"Serve the Lord with gladness; Come before His presence with singing" (Psalm 100:2 NKJV).

I spent a lot of time with my maternal grandparents when I was growing up in Ohio. One of the qualities that I most admired about my grandparents was their volunteerism. For many years, they served in my private school's thrift shops, which provided money to the school for scholarships and other expenses. My grandparents managed one location and staffed the other as necessary, and if I am remembering correctly, they would volunteer two or three days a week.

As a child, I watched my grandmother sit in the sorting room and go through donations hour after hour while my grandfather tinkered with items that needed fixed and put things away for her. My sister and I especially enjoyed helping as we got to make sure that the donated toys worked and also because we got first dibs on the much-desired accessories for our fashion dolls. Our family also helped by testing donated board games to make sure all the pieces were there. Those were fun, memorable times.

I do not remember my grandparents ever complaining about the hard work or the lack of recognition. In fact, they served with joy and excitement. I know now that it wasn't as much the work they enjoyed as it was giving back to God by helping people. They served from hearts of gratitude for His provision in their life and from the generous mercy that they felt for others. This gratitude and mercy generated the joyful and gracious attitudes which flowed out of them, touching anyone they met. I am so thankful that I got to be one of those influenced by their kind example.

> "Each of you should use whatever gift you have received to serve others, as faithful stewards of God's grace in its various forms. If anyone speaks, they should do so as one who speaks the very words of God. If anyone serves, they should do so with the strength God provides, so that in all things God may be praised through Jesus Christ. To him be the glory and the power for ever and ever. Amen" (1 Peter 4:10-11 NIV).

Spiritual Pruning

> "I am the Real Vine and my Father is the Farmer. He cuts off every branch of me that doesn't bear grapes. And every branch that is grape-bearing he prunes back so it will bear even more" (John 15:1-2 MSG).

Unless you are a gardener, it is hard to imagine how cutting away something makes the plant more productive, but it does. Cutting away the dead, unproductive branches enables the plant to concentrate its energy and its resources on fruit production. Otherwise, the dead, unproductive parts will continue to drain these away from the rest of the plant.

Spiritually speaking, I have known this situation to be true, especially in the area of service. When I was a young woman, I was passionate for the church and the kingdom. Since I was also a pastor's wife and a church secretary, this kind of active service was pretty much expected, especially when no other volunteers could be found.

In those days, I had lots of energy and was happy to help. However, it all caught up with me, and I realized I was spread too thin. With no energy, I was no longer happy or excited to help. My attitude reflected the fact that I dreaded many activities. My home life and my spiritual walk were negatively affected, and I was no longer bearing fruit or attracting souls to the kingdom.

God saw my plight and started pruning back my activity. I had to learn to give up things I'd been involved in for a long time. I also had to begin saying no to the ministries to which I felt God wasn't leading me. In the process, I discovered new, exciting areas of ministry which gave me energy instead of constantly draining it from me.

Pruning can be a painful experience, but it is necessary to grow spiritually and to lead others to salvation. We can't be effective disciples when we are always exhausted. God, our Master Gardner, knows the best way to prune us; if we place our care in His hands, He will give us the energy we need to grow.

> "There has never been the slightest doubt in my mind that the God who started this great work in you would keep at it and bring it to a flourishing finish on the very day Christ Jesus appears" (Philippians 1:6 MSG).

What's in Your Glass?

> "Rejoice always; pray without ceasing; in everything give thanks; for this is God's will for you in Christ Jesus" (1 Thessalonians 5:16-18 NASB).

Giving thanks for everything is not the easiest commandment to live by, especially during hard times. There are some people I know who always see the good in things; they are said to be optimists and see a glass as half full. Others I know are pessimistic, always seeing the glass as half empty.

I saw a social media post once that said something profound about the half-full or half-empty debate: "Be thankful that you have a glass to fill." This is a powerful and true statement. We should indeed be thankful that we have a glass—that is, that we were given a free will and choices to make as to what we put in our hearts and our minds. With choices come responsibility though. We can fill our hearts with heavenly things or worldly things, with praise or with grumbling, with anxiety or with peace.

What we decide to put in our hearts, however, will be revealed to others by our actions and words. Luke 6:45 tells us that if we store up evil, we will speak evil, and if we store up good, we will speak good. Ephesians 4:29 tells us that we should make sure that what we say builds others up and benefits those who listen. Proverbs 21:23 (ESV) is straightforward about this: "Whoever keeps his mouth and his tongue keeps himself out of trouble."

Thankfully, our God understands that we frequently mess up and offers to empty and clean our glasses when we humbly ask Him to do so. Micah 7:18-19 says that He will mercifully empty our glass's contents into the sea. He then gives us a clean glass and a new opportunity to fill it with goodness.

> "For as high as the heavens are above the earth, so great is his love for those who fear him; as far as the east is from the west, so far has He removed our transgressions from us" (Psalm 103:11-12 NIV).

A Tale of Two Dishes

> "You ask and do not receive, because you ask wrongly, to spend it on your passions" (James 4:3 ESV).

I have two male cats at my house that I dearly love. They were both adopted from shelters, but not at the same time. The first was adopted at an older age about five years ago; the second we adopted at a young age about two years ago. To our dismay, however, they have yet to become friends. This is a common problem among cat owners, as cats can be possessive and thus compete over ownership of everything, including their owners.

Besides the floor space around the sunniest window in my house, one particular area my cats compete over is food dishes. Each time I feed them, I use the same food from the same can with the same spoon. I put the food dishes down about a foot apart from each other, and the cats usually go to the same dishes each time. They always start out that way at least, but inevitably, my older cat will leave his dish and try to go for my younger cat's dish. The younger cat doesn't know enough to just switch dishes, so if I don't correct the older cat, the younger one will hiss or resort to just eating dry food. The irony is that my older cat's eyes are much bigger than his stomach, and he can't hold it all, to put it delicately. So if he succeeds in eating two dishes of food, he ultimately retains none of it and goes hungry.

I think about how silly this is every time it happens, and I instantly wonder if that is how we appear to God. He gives us blessings, and He gives our neighbor blessings, but how often do we overlook our own to covet our neighbor's? Our blessings come from the same source, our benevolent heavenly Father, who knows each of us down to the number of hairs on our heads. He gives us what we need when we need it, and He rewards us with blessings that are appropriate when we can handle them.

We get into trouble when we decide to take matters into our own hands. People live in big, empty houses because they can't afford to furnish them, and often they lose them. People get arrested for embezzling money to buy whatever they thought they needed. Marriages crumble and families are torn apart over credit card debt or affairs.

It is a slippery slope we climb when we take our focus off of God's blessings and obsess over what we want. We need to remember that taking action to get what we want often costs us and may cost other people around us as well. Unfortunately, it often costs us more than we ever wanted to pay.

"But each person is tempted when he is lured and enticed by his own desire. Then desire when it has conceived gives birth to sin, and sin when it is fully grown brings forth death" (James 1:14-15 ESV).

From His Hands

"Every good and perfect gift is from above, coming down from the Father of the heavenly lights, who does not change like shifting shadows" (James 1:17 NIV).

"**G**reat Is Thy Faithfulness,²" is a hymn that many of us grew up singing in church services. With a hymn this familiar, we may find ourselves singing the words and not paying attention to the meaning, but in so doing, we can totally miss the message and the beauty of the inspired words.

One such powerful gem that I noticed in this hymn was the lyric "All I have needed Thy hand hath provided." It is one thing to think about God providing for our needs; it is another altogether to picture Him handing it to us personally with His own hands. This powerful vision shows how much He loves us and how He faithfully provides for us by giving us what we need when we need it. It also keeps us mindful that our blessings came from God and hopefully reminds us to do our best to manage them wisely.

While God has truly given us many great blessings, it is our choice as to how we honor Him with these gifts. By being good stewards, we bless Him and others with our own two hands.

"His master replied, 'Well done, good and faithful servant! You have been faithful with a few things; I will put you in charge of many things. Come and share your master's happiness!'" (Matthew 25:21 NIV).

The Beauty of Fall

"The heavens declare the glory of God; the skies proclaim the work of His hands" (Psalm 19:1 NIV).

The first day of fall is just ahead. It's a magical time here in East Tennessee when the leaves change from green to vibrant shades of yellow, orange, brown, and red. When the Smoky Mountains are covered in their beautiful patterns, it can take our breath away.

A friend of mine once told me that she was brought to tears by the sight of colorful leaves against a gorgeous sunrise while driving to work one morning. She said the awesome sight compelled her to praise God for His beautiful handiwork. In response, I asked her, "Who do you think He painted it for?" Her eyes teared up again as she realized the answer: "God did it for us, for all of us." In both instances, she was truly touched by the love of God.

Just as a painting connects the artist, its subject, and its admirers, so it is with God and His creation. Beautiful displays in nature, such as the colorful leaves and the mighty ocean, make us feel especially connected to God. Our souls are drawn to Him with wonder, joy, and gratitude as we behold His awesome handiwork. Thus, nature has fulfilled its divine purpose, bringing glory to the Creator and providing a wondrous home for His children.

"You will live in joy and peace. The mountains and hills, the trees of the field—all the world around you—will rejoice. Where once were thorns, fir trees will grow; where briars grew, the myrtle trees will sprout up. This miracle will make the Lord's name very great and be an everlasting sign of God's power and love" (Isaiah 55:12-13 TLB).

A Rainbow of Hope

> "When I send clouds over the earth, the rainbow will appear in the clouds, and I will remember my covenant with you and with all living creatures. Never again will the floodwaters destroy all life" (Genesis 9:14-15 NLT).

One night while driving home, I came out of a blind curve, and a beautiful, vibrant rainbow appeared in front of me. It was so awesome that I could almost hear the Hallelujah Chorus playing in my ear.

We know from the Bible that the rainbow appeared as God's signature on His promise to never flood the entire earth again. It is an ancient Biblical symbol which continues to appear to this day to all of us, no matter who we are or where we live on the planet.

God's rainbow is a symbol of His love, joy, hope, and peace. During hard times, we can find peace in God's promise to always be with us. When we grieve, we can lift our eyes to the rainbow and remember there is joy beyond our sorrow and pain. When our eyes are swollen from tears and our hearts are broken, we can take hope in remembering that God's light is so powerful that it can shine through the clouds of our darkest and fiercest storms and form a beautiful rainbow.

God is our loving redeemer who works everything out for our good according to His purpose. He transforms our brokenness into strength, our sorrows into joy, and our tests into testimonies. We are living examples of His faithfulness, and we bring Him glory and honor by sharing our redemption stories with others.

> "'Return to your home, and declare how much God has done for you.' And he went away, proclaiming throughout the whole city how much Jesus had done for him" (Luke 8:39 ESV).

Curling Up with the Father

♡

"In peace I will both lie down and sleep; for you alone,
O Lord, make me dwell in safety" (Psalm 4:8 ESV).

When my daughter was little, my favorite time of the day was bedtime, not because she was such a handful that I couldn't wait for her to go to sleep but because I got to spend one-on-one time with her. We would talk to each other, read books together, and listen to music. I cherished it so much that I probably rocked her to sleep every night for the first two or three years of her life. It was a blessing to hold her in my arms and watch her sleep peacefully.

She's grown up now, and so these opportunities are limited to rocking other mothers' babies in the church nursery, opportunities which don't happen often, so I treasure them. I adore snuggling with the babies while I pray God's protection over them.

This is the picture I get when I think of God as Father. I envision feeling free and safe to approach God as a child would her father. I picture climbing up in His lap and letting Him hold me and then snuggling in to hear His heartbeat and feel His presence and His warm embrace. I imagine having a conversation with Him, telling Him how much I love and appreciate Him, sharing my daily concerns, and listening to His wise counsel. I dream of falling asleep in His arms where I sleep peacefully, knowing He is awake and watching over me.

I believe this type of relationship is what God wants as well. Psalm 22:3 says that God is enthroned in the praises of His people. Another version (the Japanese Bible) translates this as "When we worship, we build a big chair for God to sit in." Jesus welcomed children to come near Him so that He could bless them, and He told those watching that everyone needs to come to Him with love and trust as children do.

To have this type of close, personal relationship, we have to get out of the throne chair of our hearts and ask Him to sit there instead. He is our King, Lord, and Father, and thus this is His rightful place in our lives. He doesn't force us to accept Him, however. Rather, He stands by patiently and waits for our invitation.

> "Look! I stand at the door and knock. If you hear my voice and open the door, I will come in, and we will share a meal together as friends" (Revelation 3:20 NLT).

The Gentle Shepherd

> "When he has brought out all his own, he goes on ahead of them, and his sheep follow him because they know his voice. But they will never follow a stranger; in fact, they will run away from him because they do not recognize a stranger's voice" (John 10:4-5 NIV).

The Amazing Race[3] is one of my favorite reality competition shows. Contestants race around the world in teams of two, hoping to win a million dollars. They search for clues which direct them to each location, and they often have to complete a challenge to receive their next clue. Since the challenges involve the culture of each country, the show is interesting and educational to watch.

During one season, the teams were located in an area of Scotland known for its sheep farming. In this leg of the race, they were given the task of directing a small flock of sheep down a hill, through a path lined with fence posts, and into a pen. The teams were not given instructions on how to do this; they had to figure it out for themselves. Most of the teams approached the sheep like they would a cattle herd, screaming and flailing their arms, pushing the sheep toward the pen. These actions spooked the sheep, causing them to jump, scatter, and run quickly in all directions. However, the teams who approached the sheep quietly and walked gently among them were able to herd the sheep as a flock down the hill, through the fence posts, and into the pen.

In the Bible, Jesus calls Himself the Good Shepherd and calls us His sheep. Unlike most of the show's contestants, He knows the best way to lead us is with tenderness. He spends time forming relationships with us so we can learn to trust Him. Once we become familiar with Him and learn to recognize His voice, He can then slowly lead us down the paths that are best for us.

The sheep scattered when the contestants tried to herd them like cattle because they were scared. Jesus does not want us to be afraid of Him, so He leads with gentle encouragement rather than force so we'll feel safe to follow Him wherever He needs us to go. Though the path we walk to heaven is not an easy one, with the help of our Good Shepherd, we are sure to arrive safely home.

> "The Lord is my shepherd. I will always have everything I need. He gives me green pastures to lie in. He leads me by calm pools of water. He restores my strength. He leads me on right paths to show that he is good" (Psalm 23:1-2 ERV).

Finding Faith to Move

> "He went in and said to them, 'Why all this commotion and wailing? The child is not dead but asleep.' But they laughed at him" (Mark 5:39-40 NIV).

I don't know about you, but it hurts my heart to read in Mark 5:40 how the people laughed at Jesus's good news. They obviously did not believe He was telling the truth. If their rejection wasn't bad enough, this story comes between two other similar stories. Previously, Jesus had rebuked the storm and then chided His disciples for their lack of faith. After this passage, Jesus visited Nazareth where He was rejected by the people of His hometown and was unable to do much because of their lack of faith.

I have heard it said that faith is believing that God is real and that He is good. Applying this definition to the examples listed above, it makes sense. If the disciples had had faith that Jesus was God, they wouldn't have been shocked that He calmed the storm. If the mourners had believed that He could heal the official's daughter, they would have rejoiced with Him and not laughed at Him. If the people of Nazareth had believed Jesus was God, He would have felt the freedom to be the teacher and healer He wanted to be among His own people.

We show God that we believe He is real and good by exercising our faith, and we show our lack of faith and trust by refusing to move. Understandably, the first step toward faith is daunting because it is a long leap followed by a trust fall. It is necessary, however, if we want to step toward spiritual growth, strength, healing, and purpose.

Our lack of faith limits what God can accomplish though us, and standing still stunts our spiritual growth. We should always be growing stronger in our relationship with God. Then hopefully, when we stand before Him one day, we will hear Him say, "Well done, my good and faithful servant" and not "My child, why did you doubt?"

> "Have I not commanded you? Be strong and courageous.
> Do not be afraid; do not be discouraged, for the Lord your
> God will be with you wherever you go" (Joshua 1:9 NIV).

Being Neighborly

> "Don't be concerned for your own good but for the good
> of others" (1 Corinthians 10:24 NLT).

My daughter and I are both introverts. We are not ones to go visit or attend parties. We tend to stay home and refuel for when we have to be out in the world again. Being social takes a great deal of energy from us.

Knowing this, I was surprised to hear my daughter had eaten lunch with a stranger in a restaurant in the mall. I don't know many extroverted people who do this, nor do I know many people who would allow a stranger to sit and eat lunch with them. She decided to do so when she noticed a young woman being watched suspiciously by men who were sitting nearby. So by sitting down with her, my daughter effectively defused the situation and made a friend in the process.

While I was amazed at what she had done, I was also sad because I would not have been able to do what she did. I know God wants Christians to be neighborly, but I am certain my shyness and fear of people would have prohibited me.

Fear versus faith is a constant battle because we have both a sin nature and a Christian nature at war within us. Fear will overcome faith unless we choose to engage our faith. When we step out in faith, God will help us accomplish what He wants us to do. Though it may feel as if we are daring to walk on water, we can take comfort in knowing that God is already standing there to receive us.

> "But I'll take the hand of those who don't know the way, who can't see where they're going. I'll be a personal guide to them, directing them through unknown country. I'll be right there to show them what roads to take, make sure they don't fall into the ditch. These are the things I'll be doing for them—sticking with them, not leaving them for a minute" (Isaiah 42:16 MSG).

Talking to the Animals

$\heartsuit$

"Then the Lord gave the donkey the ability to speak. 'What have I done to you that deserves your beating me three times?' it asked Balaam" (Numbers 22:28 NLT).

In June 2018, a well-known gorilla named Koko passed away. Koko was famous for being fluent in sign language, both understanding it and responding with it. Koko was also famous for her relationship with children's television host Fred Rogers. In recorded videos of them together, it is amazing to see how Mr. Rogers remained calm while this huge gorilla continually touched his arms and hugged him as gently as she could. She would sign to him that she loved him, and he responded the same in both sign and voice. The two developed a special friendship, and they shared several visits together.

With the exception of special animals like Balaam's donkey and Koko, animals aren't usually able to speak to us. Therefore, communicating with them is not an easy task. Generally, we use gestures and voice inflections to speak to them, and they respond with their eyes and body gestures. Nevertheless, we still tend to have one-sided, deep conversations with them, even asking them questions as if they could answer us. Since they can't talk back and they look at us with eyes full of love, they are usually good listeners.

We have the same type of communication issues with God. We can talk to Him, and He does hear us, but He doesn't usually respond in an audible voice. Instead, we hear Him in our souls by way of a thought accompanied by a feeling. This feeling is the Holy Spirit confirming that God is speaking to us. The Holy Spirit also intercedes for us, translating our thoughts into words to share with the Father. We can communicate with our most holy heavenly Father in a close and personal way because the Holy Spirit is at work inside us.

"And I [Jesus] will ask the Father, and he will give you another advocate to help you and be with you forever—the Spirit of truth. The world cannot accept him, because it neither sees him nor knows him. But you know him, for he lives with you and will be in you" (John 14:16-17 NIV).

The Pain of Separation

"The fear and dread of you will fall on all the beasts of the earth, and on all the birds in the sky, on every creature that moves along the ground, and on all the fish in the sea; they are given into your hands" (Genesis 9:2 NIV).

I watched a video yesterday featuring zoo animals interacting with a child through the glass window of the animals' enclosure. Sometimes the animals would chase the child back and forth, and other times they put their paw up to the child's hand on the glass. In another video I watched, a clever monkey used hand signals to show a woman how to share her drink with him. He pointed to a corner of the glass where there was a small crack. When she poured her drink into that corner, it flowed around to the other side where the monkey could drink it.

These interactions between animals and people fascinate me. They always make me wonder what it would be like not to need the glass. I think it would be fun to cuddle with a lion and play with an otter. Interactions such as these remind me of the Garden of Eden when humans and animals were able to interact freely.

As the animals are separated from us, so are we separated from God. God walked with man in the Garden before sin. However, when humans sinned and were thrown out of the Garden, God's glory was too powerful for us to behold. Jesus graciously bridged this gap for us, and we can now connect with Him through the Holy Spirit who intercedes for us on our behalf. We won't physically be able to be in God's presence again until we are in heaven, at which time we will be able to walk with Him and play with the wild animals without any fear or need for protection. Won't that be wonderful!

> "For now we see in a mirror dimly, but then face to face. Now I know in part; then I shall know fully, even as I have been fully known" (1 Corinthians 13:12 ESV).

In His Image

> "So God created mankind in his own image, in the image of God he created them; male and female he created them" (Genesis 1:27 NIV).

In our staff devotion this morning, we talked about being *eikons* of Christ. Our devotion book translated this Greek word as "image." Out of curiosity, I looked up the modern English spelling of the word, *icon*, and it is defined as a representation of something.

When I saw first saw the word, my modern brain instantly went to the icons we have on our phone and computer screens. When I applied the definition, the name fit since they are pictures representing programs in our devices' memories. They are shortcuts we use to easily access the programs to which they are connected.

As I continued this train of thought, it occurred to me that an icon is only as good as the power behind it and applied to it. A computer icon's power comes from the program it represents. It is activated by clicking on it with our computer mouse or tapping on it with our finger. Without a program or way to activate it, the icon just takes up space on our screen.

So for us to be an active icon representing Christ, we have to be connected to His power and learn to apply it. The power He provides is the difference between an active Christian and an inactive one and between a useful Christian and a useless one. The key is our staying plugged in to Him through scripture, prayer, worship, and a growing relationship. If we want to be true and faithful representatives of Christ who share His love with others, we have to take time each day to connect to Him and let Him charge our spiritual batteries.

> "I am the vine; you are the branches. If you remain in me and I in you, you will bear much fruit; apart from me you can do nothing" (John 15:5 NIV).

Trip of Our Lifetime

> "The lookout reported, 'He has reached them, but he isn't coming back either. The driving is like that of Jehu son of Nimshi—he drives like a maniac'" (2 Kings 9:20 NIV).

When we first learn to drive, we have to train ourselves to pay attention to a lot of things. We have to watch for traffic lights, road signs, construction, pedestrians, bikers, animals, and more. After we've been driving a while though, we often find ourselves on autopilot, arriving at our destination without remembering the trip—that is, until we go someplace unfamiliar like a different city or country. In those cases, we may often miss signs and take risky chances with u-turns, driving the wrong way on one-way streets and across medians, which puts us and our passengers in danger.

This ebb and flow of driving can also apply to our Christian walk. When we first become Christians, we begin learning how to walk with Him. We learn how to notice His voice as His Holy Spirit speaks to us, and we learn how to speak to Him in prayer. We learn to read and study the Bible, and we learn how to worship Him. We learn the benefits of being part of a supportive community of Christian believers and of sharing God's love with others.

Once we've been Christians for a while, however, we can easily go on autopilot, which means going through the motions of a Christian walk without feeling any real desire or passion. During those times, we tend to look at our Bibles only when we are in church, pray only when we're asked to do so, and support His ministries only in lip service. We are too busy to make spending quality time with God a priority. We often go this way for a while until we are spurred on by conviction or a reprimand, or until we feel He's our only hope in a crisis.

Coasting through our Christian walk is no way to live because we miss so much that God has to offer. He created us to walk with Him daily, not to just check in with Him occasionally. This relationship is not one-sided or routine. It is a relationship with a Holy God, requiring commitment and a connection to stay passionate, loved, and fulfilled together. He desires to walk our life's journey with us, and He wants so much to enjoy our companionship and reveal wonderful sights along the way. This eternal privilege cost Him dearly, and we would do well to always honor His sacrifice.

> "God, you did everything you promised, and I'm thanking you with all my heart. You pulled me from the brink of death, my feet from the cliff-edge of doom. Now I stroll at leisure with God in the sunlit fields of life" (Psalm 56:12-13 MSG).

Lessons from the Truck

> "From heaven the Lord looks down and sees all mankind; from his dwelling place he watches all who live on earth" (Psalm 33:13-14 NIV).

As I drove a moving truck from North Carolina to Tennessee, I gained a whole new perspective on highway driving. From my higher vantage point in the truck, I could see much farther ahead than I could from my car. To my dismay, I also realized that we work our guardian angels hard when we are driving. I can't tell you how many times I watched someone get cut off when another driver changed lanes or wouldn't pull over at a lane merge. It was pretty scary.

Secondly, I learned that it takes longer for a truck to stop and to get moving. I knew that fact while I was driving my car, but I didn't really understand until I was trying to drive the truck. What's worse is that I was following my daughter, who was driving my newly purchased car. Since she had not driven a truck, she didn't know to speed up or slow down at appropriate times, and I found myself working hard not to run over her and wreck my car.

Thirdly, I learned that I was a lot more concerned about what was ahead of me than behind me. Though I know it is important to look behind when changing lanes or stopping, I found myself looking ahead more often because the truck had no rearview mirror and the rear window was blocked by the trailer. Furthermore, by looking ahead, I could prepare for hills and valleys as they approached so I could adjust my speed.

These lessons can be applied spiritually as well. First, God taught me there is a huge difference in our views. He has a much better and different perspective on my life than I have, and so I should trust Him to look out for me. There is no blind spot in His vision. Secondly, He taught me to trust His perfect timing. He knows what is ahead and can best prepare me for it. Thirdly, He showed me how it is better to simply glance back at the past while paying attention to the present and looking forward to the future. After all, we are traveling forward, not backwards. We have a heavenly destination ahead, and God is the perfect guide to get us there.

"Forgetting what is behind and straining toward what is ahead, I press on toward the goal to win the prize for which God has called me heavenward in Christ Jesus" (Philippians 3:13b-14 NIV).

That Overwhelmed Feeling

"So my spirit grows faint within me; my heart within me is dismayed" (Psalm 143:4 NIV).

In my lifetime, I have moved over twenty-five times. Many of the moves were Army transfers because both my father and stepfather were in the Army. Later on, the moves were because my husband and I continually sought out cheaper rentals when we were young and newly married. With all this relocating, I should be a pro at packing and moving; however, it is never easy.

The worse part for me is unpacking. Since moving is exhausting, it takes a while to find the energy to unpack and decide where to put everything. So for several days, we live out of boxes and are surrounded by boxes. Since there seems to be no end to it, the stress keeps piling up.

All of us at one time or another have felt overwhelmed from too many tasks or expectations. Sometimes this feeling is because we have taken on too much, and other times it is because too much has been thrust upon us. Despite the cause, the basic reason we become overwhelmed is that we reach the end of ourselves—the end of our strength, our time, our resources, our stamina, our health, etc. At this point, many of us remember to call upon God and ask for help because we realize our need for His supernatural strength, knowledge, and wisdom to move forward. He answers us by opening our eyes to the solution, by giving us the strength to stand or the wisdom and serenity to better manage tasks. Unfortunately, if we had been wise, we would have asked God for help earlier.

How frustrating it must be for God to watch us struggle while we stubbornly try to do everything on our own. By deciding to go it alone, we force our all-powerful God to stand by and watch until we invite Him to help. We seem to have it backwards. We should seek Him first and allow Him to work through us before we become overwhelmed.

"Commit your way to the Lord; trust in him, and he will act" (Psalm 37:5 ESV).

Do We Only Share Our Leftovers?

⸻ ♡ ⸻

"'Try offering them to your governor! Would he be pleased with you? Would he accept you?' says the Lord Almighty" (Malachi 1:8b NIV).

I have been involved in many churches in my lifetime in several states ranging from Texas to Ohio. If I counted correctly, I can think of more than ten churches that I or my family have attended or worked for during my lifetime. Every church and congregation is different, but some have things in common.

The most interesting commonality that I have come across is that congregations tend to drop off their old technology at church. For some odd reason, people think the church is always in need of old computers, TVs, cassette players, VCR's, camcorders, cameras, and even 8-track players. I venture to guess that if we stepped into any random church in America, the secretary could point us to an old TV that was dropped off at the church—and usually it is a huge one with a big screen that doesn't project any more.

As I walked past two such TVs in separate churches in the last three days, God gave me this thought each time: Do we bring Him what is left over of ourselves or do we bring Him our best? Specifically, I thought of prayer, which is something I struggle with often. I questioned, "Do I give Him prioritized quality time, or do I give Him what is left of my time and my energy?" The same can be asked of many other facets of the Christian walk. What about our service, our abilities, our giftedness, our worship, our blessings? Do we give Him our best or what is left?

The thought begs the question, what if God withheld His best from us? What if He had decided that humanity was not worth redeeming and He refused to let His Son come to earth to save us? If He allowed us to live, we would be forever lost, sentenced to a lifetime of stumbling around in perpetual, spiritual darkness with no hope for anything changing.

God shared His best with us, so why do we only give Him our leftovers? If we love Him as much as we say we do, shouldn't we want to honor Him in the best way possible? God will certainly honor our sacrifice when we lay our best on the altar.

"Give, and it will be given to you. A good measure, pressed down, shaken together and running over, will be poured into your lap. For with the measure you use, it will be measured to you" (Luke 6:38 NIV).

The Old Church

"Let them construct a Sanctuary for me so that I can live among them" (Exodus 25:8 MSG).

On one of my trips to Dayton, Ohio, where I grew up, I took the opportunity to show my daughter some of the sites from my childhood. I showed her my grandparents' home where I spent much of my childhood, an apartment complex where my mom and my sister and I lived for a little while, and the church my family used to attend. The neighborhood I grew up in was an older one when I was being raised there; the houses were close to a hundred years old then. Therefore, I was not surprised by their current deteriorated condition, but I was sad to see it.

The hardest site to see was the church where I grew up. I had not seen it in 20 years, and it was now abandoned, empty, falling apart, and barely standing up in the middle of a broken-down neighborhood. My family told me later that the current congregation had moved out of the building and now met in a different location. Though in my heart I totally understood their decision to leave, I grieved the fact that the building was no longer alive with people and ministry. Unfortunately, like everyone and everything else, it aged with the times and no longer suited the needs of its people.

The dilapidated church made me think about the state of my heart.

I hope when God looks at my soul, He doesn't see a shadow of what it once was when I was younger, energetic, and passionate. I hope He sees a growing and thriving heart, one in which He enjoys living. I hope it is still as sacred and holy as it was when I first invited Him to live there.

It is important to frequently take the time to closely evaluate the state of our hearts, for whatever state our hearts are in directly reflects the state of our relationship with God. If our hearts are no longer a place where we feel God at work in our lives, then we need to do some spiritual maintenance and housecleaning. We need to confess whatever stands between us and God and ask Him to clear it away with forgiveness to revitalize our relationship. Thus when God looks at our hearts, He won't see a dilapidated church building where a live and growing faith used to be, but He will see a thriving heart fed by the living water of the Holy Spirit.

> "Since you have heard about Jesus and have learned the truth that comes from him, throw off your old sinful nature and your former way of life, which is corrupted by lust and deception. Instead, let the Spirit renew your thoughts and attitudes. Put on your new nature, created to be like God—truly righteous and holy" (Ephesians 4:21-24 NLT).

One Faithful Step

> "'If you can?' said Jesus. 'Everything is possible for one who believes.' Immediately the boy's father exclaimed, 'I do believe; help me overcome my unbelief!'" (Mark 9:23-24 NIV).

How many times have we been where this desperate father was? Standing on the shore of unbelief but wanting to get to the other side without having to walk through the turbulent water between them. The water we face is made up of both fear and faith—fear of the unknown and a faith in our unseen God who wants to help us navigate the unknown.

The father knew that his boy was dying, and he knew that Jesus could help him, yet, he struggled within himself to trust. His admitting his weakness and asking Jesus to help his unbelief was His first step out of fear into faith.

From the beginning of time, God has required us to step out in faith towards him. Noah had to build an ark before he even saw any rain. The Israelites had to step into the Red Sea and again into the Jordan River to get to freedom. Gideon had to step out with a small army to fight a large one. Naaman had to wash himself in the Jordan to receive healing from leprosy. Teenage Mary had to accept her call from the angel to become the mother of Jesus. The blind man had to admit that he believed Jesus could heal him before Jesus would do so. The list goes on and on.

God could do all of these miracles in His own power, but He wants us to join Him in His miracles. He wants us to see Him and not just His work. When we cooperate and invest our faith in Him, He works through our weaknesses so we can know firsthand what He is able to accomplish through us. We may need to first admit our doubts and seek His help to believe, but He will honor our effort and help us to get through whatever we are facing. Any little step in His direction will be noticed and honored by God, who patiently waits for us to join Him.

> "And without faith it is impossible to please God, because anyone who comes to him must believe that he exists and that he rewards those who earnestly seek him" (Hebrews 11:6 NIV).

Church Shopping

"The Lord looks down from heaven on the children of man, to see if there are any who understand, who seek after God. They have all turned aside; together they have become corrupt; there is none who does good, not even one" (Psalm 14:2-3 ESV).

These days, most of us do our shopping and searching online. Our schedules are packed full of activity, and we have little free time. Therefore, it is convenient to do everything from our phones, which we can do from any place and at any time. We can shop for groceries, cars, and houses; look for sporting activities for our kids; do our banking; attend college; search for local events and restaurants; and on and on. It is rare for us to get in our car, go from place to place, and walk into a business. Our worse-case scenario is maybe having to talk to someone in person or on the phone.

The same is true for the modern-day church search. Today, people shop for churches by going online and researching them. They look at the church's website and social media to see if the church's views align with their own. They watch sermons to see if they like the pastor. Then if they decide they like a church, instead of visiting, they may choose to watch or listen to sermons online. Again, they can do that at any time and from anywhere, and they don't have to interact with people.

Unfortunately, there is a serious side effect to online attendance. The children of parents who only attend church online get no real church experience at all. They lose out on learning godly values and the necessity of having a personal relationship with God. They don't make church friends or meet adult mentors who could become a valuable support system for them both now and in the future. Since their parents didn't make church a priority, the children learned that whatever the family did on Sundays was more important than worshipping, serving, or learning about God through a church.

It has been said that we are living in a post-Christian society, and it is easy to see why. For if parents are solely internet church attenders, then their children may never actually attend church. This situation presents a challenge to Christians today because we have to discern from God how to reach this technology-driven, lost generation of children with the love of Christ. It is vitally important that we do so, for if we don't, future generations may never fully know God's love for them or find the value of having a supportive Christian community.

"I, the Lord, will teach your children, and they will have real peace" (Isaiah 54:13 ERV).

A Renewed Mind

"I do not understand what I do. For what I want to do I do not do, but what I hate I do. And if I do what I do not want to do, I agree that the law is good. As it is, it is no longer I myself who do it, but it is sin living in me" (Romans 7:15-16 NIV).

Many of us make New Year's resolutions. Some want to get healthy, read their Bible through in a year, get out of debt, cut down time spent on social media, and other similar goals. I have made some of these too, but apparently, I am not so resolute in my decisions because I usually don't even start them. The fact is, it takes a lot of mental energy to integrate new habits because they involve redirecting our thinking and making choices each day. In my case, I am often worn out from the holidays, so I don't find the energy or strength to pursue making changes.

In thinking about my well-intentioned but unstarted resolutions, I told God this morning that I wish I had a "reset" or "renew" button on my brain. I wouldn't want to forget anything, but I would love to press a button and have a good new habit or a fresh start instantly installed in my brain. I could bypass all the struggle, and the habit would instantly be there and available to me.

As I thought more about it this morning, God spoke to me through a vision. He showed me a picture of my brain, and then suddenly I saw His blood pouring over it. I was not afraid or even grossed out, but rather I was at peace. Afterwards, I felt clean and renewed, and my thinking was sharper than it had been in a long time. Then He peacefully spoke to my heart, saying, "Dear One, this is how you renew your mind. You give it to me so I can wash it clean with the blood My Son shed for you."

This vision reminded me that through Jesus, God has already done what is necessary for us to get a renewed mind; we just have to ask. If we wholeheartedly seek Him and allow Him to work in our hearts, He will pour His Spirit into us and renew us. With His power, we can overcome the barriers we find ourselves up against on the way to success. Moreover, when we work with God, we can achieve bigger and better things than we ever imagined possible.

"I can do all this through him who gives me strength" (Philippians 4:13 NIV).

A Codependent's Journey

"Am I now trying to win the approval of human beings, or of God? Or am I trying to please people? If I were still trying to please people, I would not be a servant of Christ" (Galatians 1:10 NIV).

One of my biggest issues on my path to self-confidence is codependency, the act of people-pleasing to an unhealthy level by letting a particular person's opinion determine our self-worth, happiness, failure, success, and love. Worse still is that we take that person's opinion as the world's opinion of us as well. Codependency is not only unhealthy, but it is also dangerous for we run the risk of falling into the hands of an evil, controlling person who takes advantage of the situation.

As a codependent person, I first relied on my family to define me and then on my husband. When he passed away, I once again looked for someone to satisfy my codependent needs. In my grief, I spent most of my time in the church where I both worked and worshipped, and unfortunately, I thus developed a codependent relationship with its people. I worked constantly trying to do everything for everyone so they would approve of me and always be happy with me. I fulfilled every available need so I would be indispensable and people would need me and feel they couldn't reject me. I took every critical word personally as a strike against my identity. I spent all my time and energy fighting a losing battle, which left me feeling like a failure. My self-esteem and confidence tanked. I found myself feeling rejected, unloved, depressed, and broken.

Thankfully, my pastor and close friends saved my life by directing me to licensed Christian therapists for help. Through regular therapy, I began to develop a healthy identity—one that was not dependent upon my perfection or wrapped up in the opinion of others. As I progressed, God used each step to draw me to Himself and show me who I was in His eyes. I discovered that I was His beloved child, and He was my good Father. I was worthy of His love, grace, and mercy, and I always would be. There was nothing I could do to sever myself from His love for me.

Finally, my dependent heart had found a resting place within the heart of God. He is now my One-to-Please, not to prove myself worthy of His love, but rather as an outpouring of my love and gratitude to Him for all He has done and is doing in my life. I will always battle codependency, but I now have a different goal. My heart's desire is to stay dependent upon God so that I never become mentally enslaved to another person again.

> "But you are a chosen people, a royal priesthood, a holy nation, God's special possession, that you may declare the praises of him who called you out of darkness into his wonderful light" (1 Peter 2:9 NIV).

Watching the Signs

$\heartsuit$

"I have told you these things, so that in me you may have peace. In this world you will have trouble. But take heart! I have overcome the world" (John 16:33 NIV).

We all face difficult times of feeling lost and confused, especially when navigating uncharted territories. Sometimes we willingly take on something new, and at other times we are thrust into it. No matter which the case is, it is not a comfortable place to linger.

I've been in this state for a while now, not knowing which way to turn or what to do in writing this devotional book. The writing process is new and exciting yet scary and confusing all at the same time. I have found myself praying really, really hard in this process, which is probably a reason God tasked me with it.

God replied by showing me the same three signs in quick succession: a cardinal, a penny, and a dime. The cardinal represents my grandmother who collected items with cardinals on them. She was a strong Christian woman who had experienced a war which took her young first husband and severely affected her second. The penny represents her husband, my grandfather, who collected wheat pennies. He was a death march survivor and a former World War II prisoner of war who fought to overcome Post-Traumatic Stress Disorder and other lasting effects from his imprisonment. The dime represents my late husband, a young preacher who bravely suffered and died from brain cancer. The dimes began appearing as I prayed for comfort from his loss.

God reminded me of these loved ones to encourage and inspire me. They all found themselves suffering hard times and chose to give God glory and to lean on Him for strength and direction. They found their power in God's grace and love. God honored their faithfulness by guiding them on their journeys. He did all of this for them, so I know He can also do it for me.

"You will keep in perfect peace all who trust in you, all whose thoughts are fixed on you! Trust in the Lord always, for the Lord God is the eternal Rock" (Isaiah 26:3-4 NLT).

Adjusting and Changing

"Immediately the Spirit impelled Him to go out into the wilderness" (Mark 1:12 NASB).

When my grandfather was released from a Japanese prison camp after World War II, he was given the choice of taking an airplane or a ship home. He was a medic in the service before being captured, and so he knew his body needed time to acclimate to life and food outside of the prison camp where he'd been held for three and a half years. Therefore, he decided it was better to take the ship home. While on the ship, he slowly adjusted himself to eating more and different food, often turning down the rich and heavy food that was offered him. His concern was validated as he saw many of his fellow former POW's become sick from overindulging.

In the Bible, the Israelites also needed time to adjust to life outside of slavery. For generations they had not been given many choices as to how they would live or what they would do because they were under the rule of the Egyptians. So when they were freed, it was a totally new life for them.

They needed the slow walk to Canaan to get the Egyptian slave mentality out of them. They had to learn to make their own decisions and to fend for themselves. They even had to learn to rest and to not work on the Sabbath. Most of all though, they needed to learn more about God and His ways, for unlike the Egyptians, God was a benevolent and loving taskmaster.

So it is with the Christian life. We start out as new Christians, and we have to adjust to living life differently. We learn to avoid sin and choose God's ways. We learn how to cultivate and develop a close relationship with God. Then we spend our lives working on this relationship in order to strengthen it, discern the will of God for our lives, and keep ourselves from sin's slavery.

Adjustments and changes are a part of life. Sometimes we have to go through times of wilderness to work something out of or into our lives. Rest assured though, we don't go alone. As the Israelites had the cloud by day and the fire by night, God is also leading us with His Holy Spirit who lives inside of us.

> "But now that you have been set free from sin and have become slaves of God, the benefit you reap leads to holiness, and the result is eternal life" (Romans 6:22 NIV).

Feeling Like a Lost Sock

"I will search for the lost and bring back the strays" (Ezekiel 34:16a NIV).

While walking to my car in my church's parking lot, I noticed a lone black sock lying on the pavement. As I walked by it, I thought about how easy it is to lose socks. They get lost in the washer, attach themselves to other clothing, fall out of our suitcases and laundry baskets, and get lost in dresser drawers. Once separated, the socks are pretty much useless unless someone pairs them with another unmatched sock or turns them into something else like a hand puppet or a beanbag.

This lost sock in the church parking lot interestingly enough reminded me of myself. When I became a widow, I felt much like a lost sock. My world completely changed in a moment. I was no longer a couple, or a wife, or a pastor's wife. I was a single mother who felt overwhelmed and alone in the world. My identity had been roughly shaken, and I felt as if I had lost my purpose and my ministry.

God, however, saw my lonely, broken state, and He raised my head and took my hand, pairing Himself to me. He gave me a new purpose and a new identity which was tied to Him and not to another person. The path I walk now is an unintended one, but it is the path created especially for me by my loving Heavenly Father.

> "After you have suffered a little while, our God, who is full of kindness through Christ, will give you his eternal glory. He personally will come and pick you up, and set you firmly in place, and make you stronger than ever" (1 Peter 5:10 TLB).

Encouraged to Encourage Others

> "He comes alongside us when we go through hard times, and before you know it, he brings us alongside someone else who is going through hard times so that we can be there for that person just as God was there for us" (2 Corinthians 1:4 MSG).

This verse reminds me of a time when I was deep into my journey with my husband's brain cancer. A friend whom I went to church with told me about a friend of hers who had gone through this same type of cancer with her husband. She wanted to set up a time when she could get us together to talk.

I was hesitant due to the fact that the friend's husband had passed away, and mine was still alive. She was at a place where I wasn't ready to go. I was still holding out hope for survival even though the doctors did not have any hope at all. My friend finally persuaded me, however, and I agreed to meet out of consideration for her.

I remember walking into the pastor's study that day to meet Judy. I was incredibly shy and nervous, but her warm smile and greeting put me at ease immediately. Soon we were talking about things that went along with this type of brain cancer that only cancer patients' spouses would understand. After a while, I finally felt safe and brave enough to ask her about the process of her husband's death and how she helped her children through it. She kindly and tenderly told me her story with a complete understanding of how hard it was for me to hear. I did not know it at the time, but I would soon be facing that situation myself. When we left together that day, we were friends, and we have kept in touch ever since then.

As Judy was there for me, I have been able to encourage others. I can easily relate to widows and widowers, both young and old. I can also relate to single parents, from both the single parent's and the child's point of view. Furthermore, I can also identify with the spouses of cancer patients and caregivers. Being able to understand the situations of so many types of people has been beneficial as a friend, a church family member, a church leader, and a writer.

As the scripture above says, God does indeed walk alongside us through trials, helping us to cope each day. He overfills us with His love and support so that we can spill love and support upon others. In so doing, we are literally being the loving arms of God.

> "If you've gotten anything at all out of following Christ,
> if his love has made any difference in your life, if being
> in a community of the Spirit means anything to you,
> if you have a heart, if you care—then do me a favor:
> Agree with each other, love each other, be deep-spirited
> friends" (Philippians 2:1-2 MSG).

My Name Is Somebody

"Then your Father, who sees what is done in secret, will reward you" (Matthew 6:4b NIV).

My church and I suffered a great loss when our dear friend Sarah died suddenly and unexpectedly. Sarah was full of joy and laughter. She loved her family and our church passionately. She was always busy serving; however, not many knew about her service because she chose to work behind the scenes.

At her funeral, the preacher told a story shared by Sarah's husband. In a conversation with her husband, Sarah mentioned a task that needed to be done and said, "Somebody ought to do that." Then she added with a grin, "I guess my name is Somebody." She was one hundred percent right: she was our church's Somebody. As the church's secretary, who also served behind the scenes, I was often privileged to see her serve. She was inspirational, doing every task joyfully and to the best of her ability. She served wholeheartedly out of her passionate love for God and the church.

As I thought about Sarah, I thought about Jesus' helpers, the disciples. The gospels mention all twelve disciples when Jesus called them, but for a few such as Thaddeus and Simon the Zealot, this was one of the only times they were mentioned. We don't know much about them or their ministries, but we do know that Jesus called them because He needed them.

Sarah, Thaddeus, Simon, and others may have worked anonymously, but they were not unseen by God. None of them escaped God's notice because He is always watching and sees everything. I know He was proud of them as He is of all His children who serve Him out of a grateful, sacrificial, and joyful heart.

"God is not unjust; he will not forget your work and the love you have shown him as you have helped his people and continue to help them" (Hebrews 6:10 NIV).

The Strength of Humility

"Now Moses was a very humble man, more humble than
anyone else on the face of the earth" (Numbers 12:3 NIV).

In Numbers 12, Moses' sister Miriam and his brother Aaron were
caught criticizing Moses because he married a Cushite wife. The
verse above was included in this account to give us insight into Moses'
character as the story progresses and God deals with Miriam and Aaron.
This statement says much about Moses and his ministry, for it was
because of his humility that God was able to make him great.

Humility can be defined as being selfless. It describes people who
are not self-centered; they think more of others than themselves. Moses
was such a man. He did not seem to be aware of greatness, nor did he
seem to have an agenda to make himself great. Instead, he seemed to be
a leader who took each day as it came, carrying forth God's commands
in leading the people.

Because of his humility, he relied on God for everything, resulting
in God being able to use him in amazing ways. The Bible says that God
and Moses were friends and that God spoke to him directly instead
of speaking to him in visions and dreams as He did to the prophets
(Numbers 12:6-8). As a friend, God also defended Moses to those who
challenged him, even Moses' siblings, Aaron and Miriam. God made it
evident to the world that He was with Moses.

Ultimately, God was able to guide Moses to lead a great number of
people out of slavery, to establish His laws for living and for worship, and
to turn these former slaves into a great nation, all of which would have
never been possible had Moses not submitted to God's direction and
leadership. We can all take a lesson from Moses: when we back off from
ourselves and become humble, we give God room to work through us.

"For all those who exalt themselves will be humbled,
and those who humble themselves will be exalted"
(Luke 14:11 NIV).

Joseph's Coats

♡

"When I was a child, I talked like a child, I thought like a child, I reasoned like a child. When I became a man, I put the ways of childhood behind me" (1 Corinthians 13:11 NIV).

A prominent story in the Old Testament is the story of Joseph, the son of Jacob and the grandson of Abraham. Many know him from the story of the colorful coat of many colors which his father gave him; however, this coat is only one of three cloaks in the story of Joseph.

The coat of many colors given to Joseph by his father as a sign of favoritism fanned the flame of jealousy among Joseph's eleven brothers. Joseph complicated the situation when he told his brothers about his dream of them bowing down to him. Eventually, when the brothers' anger overcame their consciences, they sold Joseph off as a slave to Ishmaelites who then sold him to Egyptians. The brothers then took the coat, dipped it in blood, and told their father that Joseph had been killed by animals.

The next time we read about a cloak, Joseph was a highly respected slave working as a household overseer in the house of Potiphar, Pharaoh's official. Pursued by Potiphar's wife, Joseph left his cloak behind in her hands as he fled her advances. Joseph still upheld his faith and obedience to God even while a slave, and therefore, out of obedience to God's commands and out of respect for Potiphar, he decided to flee rather than to sin. Potiphar's wife's pride was wounded, and she used the cloak to prove her lie that Joseph had pursued her. Potiphar believed her lie, a belief that landed the innocent Joseph in prison.

Finally, the third time we read about Joseph's cloak, he was out of prison and given royal clothes, which would have included a cloak, along with the king's signet ring as signs he was second in command to Pharaoh himself. Joseph's journey from Israelite kid brother, to a slave, to a prisoner, to second in command in Egypt could have only been brought about as a result of God's faithful work in Joseph's life. Joseph showed great respect, integrity, and honor for God, and God enabled Joseph to rise to authority, making a good result happen out of a horrible situation. At the end, when Joseph's brothers bowed down to him as his dream had predicted, Joseph was no longer proud of it, but he instead focused on restoring his family, which was a huge leap in maturity for Joseph.

Sometimes we find ourselves wearing different types of cloaks—ones we put on ourselves and ones that others put upon us. However, as we can see from Joseph's story, God can use our cloak experiences to train and prepare us for His future purposes and to teach us how to fully depend on Him. When we endure these difficult times, we will one day find ourselves involved in a fulfilling ministry directly suited to our gifts and experiences, and we will also have a powerful testimony about how God worked in our lives to get us there.

> "'My thoughts are nothing like your thoughts,' says the Lord. 'And my ways are far beyond anything you could imagine'" (Isaiah 55:8 NLT).

Having a Stiff Neck

"'I have seen these people,' the Lord said to Moses, 'and they are a stiff-necked people'" (Exodus 32:9 NIV).

If you've ever had a stiff neck, you know how miserable it is. You either fight through the pain to turn it, or you turn your whole body to avoid the pain, or you just don't look at all. Every time you turn it, it produces a new experience in pain.

In this Exodus verse, God called the Israelite people stiff-necked. They were stuck in one direction and were too stubborn to change. They set their minds on going back to the familiar ways of Egypt even though they would be slaves. Furthermore, they continued to worship idols rather than worship the one, true God who had freed them (Numbers 14:3-4).

As they prepared to enter the land of Canaan, Moses sent twelve men ahead to spy out the land and its inhabitants. All twelve of the spies reported the land was fruitful; however, only two recommended they enter it. These two men, Joshua and Caleb, trusted God to help the Israelites conquer the terrifying people who were living there, yet the Israelites gave in to fear and sided with the majority, a decision which reflected their lack of faith and trust in God. Despite the fact that the Israelites were close enough to enter the land God had promised them, God forced them to wander in the wilderness an additional 40 years as a consequence of their rebellion.

Following God by faith is a choice. In order to discern His directions, we must first yield to Him and ask Him to show us the way. We have to then remain sensitive to the Holy Spirit in order to hear God's answer. If we become stiff-necked and choose to go our own way, however, there is a good chance the path we walk will lead us to disaster.

> "I will instruct you and teach you in the way you should go; I will counsel you with my eye upon you. Be not like a horse or a mule, without understanding, which must be curbed with bit and bridle, or it will not stay near you" (Psalm 32:8-9 ESV).

Who Is God to You?

> "And without faith it is impossible to please him, for whoever would draw near to God must believe that he exists and that he rewards those who seek him" (Hebrews 11:6 ESV).

If I surveyed one hundred people asking them to describe God, I would get many different answers. We all lead separate lives influenced by many factors; therefore, we each have our own description of God based upon our experience with Him.

As I thought about this idea recently, it occurred to me that the truth of how we really see God is to ask ourselves how He feels about us. For instance, people who see God as loving might say that He loves them. People who are angry with God might say that He hates them. People who are confused by God might say they are unsure how He feels about them. Since we can't physically see Him, our perceptions are based upon our history with Him.

So if we want to overcome a bad point of view or enhance a good point of view, we need to pay attention to the testimonies of others instead of relying on our own perceptions. One way we do this is by opening our Bibles to read the accounts of others who shared personal experiences with God. We can also listen to the testimonies of our fellow believers through one-on-one conversations and group discussions.

Despite how we see God, it is important to believe that God loves us. He is love, which is why He created us and why He continues to seek a relationship with us. This unconditional love, which we could never earn, is the foundation upon which our relationship, our perceptions, and our faith are built.

"I want you woven into a tapestry of love, in touch with everything there is to know of God" (Colossians 2:2 MSG).

No Fear in Love

"I sought the Lord, and he answered me; he delivered me from all my fears" (Psalm 34:4 NIV).

I grew up living in fear. Shy and soft-spoken, I was an easy target for bullies. It wasn't just bullies who frightened me though; it was people in general. I was introverted and felt terribly awkward and uncomfortable around people until I got to know them. Even then, I stayed quiet most of the time. People simply scared me.

This fear carried over into my spiritual life as well. In church when I was growing up, it seemed that most preachers used scare tactics to save people from hell. They preached long sermons full of fire and brimstone, making God seem angry all the time and fixating on eternal punishment for our sins. I grew up afraid of God, and I made a salvation decision so I would not go to hell.

Many of my life experiences after that decision were traumatic. I did not feel safe, nor did I know how to process all the trauma that happened in my life. So as a teenager and young adult, I felt punished, and I was convinced that God enjoyed tormenting me. I did not feel His love, and I served Him out of fear. I hoped that one day the balance would shift my way, and God would no longer want to hurt me. My future seemed bleak.

Graciously, God did not give up on me. He pursued me with His love and tenderly brought me into the light. I clearly saw the truth as spoken in 1 John 4: God is love and there is no fear in love. I realized my fear had driven a wedge between me and God, which was surely as our enemy intended. Thankfully, God's love broke through all my barriers and drew me to Himself and bonded me with Him. I found hope, joy, and security as I learned to rest in His love.

I am able to write this today because He drove out my fear. He gave me the confidence and the courage I needed to finally speak—not only to speak, but to do it boldly and loudly enough for everyone to hear.

> "Such love has no fear, because perfect love expels all fear. If we are afraid, it is for fear of punishment, and this shows that we have not fully experienced his perfect love" (1 John 4:18 NLT).

Who Determines Your Value?

"Be devoted to one another in love. Honor one another above yourselves" (Romans 12:10 NIV).

There is no denying it: I am not an athlete. I am not competitive nor am I gifted with athletic ability. I was always chosen last for teams, which is not really a choice but rather an assignment. It was usually not a secret how the teams felt about being stuck with me. I felt defeated before I even tried.

My daughter is facing this type of issue in the adult world right now as she is trying to find a job. Like most people, she finds interviewing nerve-wracking as it requires sitting in front of possible employers who may or may not hire her. She's been waiting to hear from interviews, and when I asked her about it one day, she told me waiting is okay because she wants a job where she is chosen for her assets and not just assigned to be another body in a chair. In other words, she wants to be an integral part of the team in order to feel valuable to her work community. She'd rather be patient if it means she'll be chosen for the right job.

People might not choose us or find us valuable, but God always does. Each of us is precious and dearly loved by Him, and He welcomes us into His family of faith. We each have a purpose in our community, and we've each been given specific gifts and talents which reveal this purpose and enable us to accomplish it. We are each special and unique in God's eyes, and we, as a faith community, would do well to always remember that when we are dealing with people.

"But you are a chosen people, a royal priesthood, a holy nation, God's special possession, that you may declare the praises of him who called you out of darkness into his wonderful light" (1 Peter 2:9 NIV).

Harmful Words

"Therefore encourage one another and build each other up,
just as in fact you are doing" (1 Thessalonians 5:11 NIV).

When I was in high school, I took a typing class—now this was not a keyboarding class, but an actual typing class on actual typewriters, the old IBM Selectric models, which were very loud machines. To grade our progress, we were required to take timed-writing tests. The grades were determined by the number of words typed less the number of mistakes divided by the number of minutes, which gave us a word-per-minute number, so the goal was to be accurate and fast.

I was not an accurate typist, and there was no way to erase mistakes as we typed; therefore, I did not make good grades. One day I will never forget, my teacher looked at me and said, "You will never be a typist." Her comment broke my heart. I felt as if a door had been slammed in my face, and I had no hope of ever rising above her assessment of me both in the classroom and in my future. I did finish the class, but I struggled the entire time.

When I got to college, I decided to give it another try and get a Secretarial Practice minor. Again, the timed-writings were the bane of my existence. I was an A-B student, and I could not get above a C in the class because of these tests. In my mind, the C reinforced my high school teacher's assessment of me and my skills, so I had no hope. However, when I went to the professor and told her that I wanted to drop the class and change my minor, she was kind to me. She told me that she thought I could make it and that I should stick with it. So I did, mostly because she had faith in me.

While I never did get above a C in timed writings, I excelled in the first word processing programs on computers and also in business forms, business writing, and other similar classes. I graduated with the degree, and I have since worked in various roles as a secretary, including the office of my college's president.

Throughout the Bible, God warns us to be careful about what we say. The words we say or write to people, especially to young people, may have a significant impact on them, much as my high school teacher's words did to me. At a time when they are figuring out their gifts, talents, abilities, and life goals, what we say can have a huge effect on their self-confidence and can, in fact, discourage them from having a relationship with God or attending church. Mentoring and guiding them are much more effective than negating their worth altogether.

As we interact with others, we would do well to keep in mind the influence that we have on them. Erring on the side of caution would be a much better decision than speaking discouraging words into someone's life.

> "The one who has knowledge uses words with restraint, and whoever has understanding is even-tempered. Even fools are thought wise if they keep silent, and discerning if they hold their tongues" (Proverbs 17:27-28 NIV).

Created to Create

> "All things were made *and* came into existence through Him; and without Him not even one thing was made that has come into being" (John 1:3 AMP).

One of my favorite classes when I was in seventh grade was a general art class. In this class, we explored different types of art by experimenting. Some of the art projects I remember doing were pottery, tie dye, batik, and printing. Since I loved being creative, I spent much time doing arts and crafts in my younger years.

This love resurfaced when I took an art therapy class several years ago. This class showed me and the other students how to explore our minds through art projects. The colors and shapes we used and the placement of things in our projects told us something about ourselves, teaching us that art is born in the heart of the artist. It was in this class that I learned to journal and discovered my gift for writing.

My art experiences remind me about God as our Creator. He originally made our intricate bodies in His image by forming us from the dust of the ground, and He continues to do so by using tiny cells. He created us to love Him, and thus we were lovingly created and put in the world He made just for us. We are outpourings of His heart, much like an artist's painting on canvas and a writer's words on paper. God, however, doesn't need tools or a canvas to create; He can create from absolutely nothing. The beautiful and complex world we live in was created with His spoken word.

Each of us is a work of art designed tenderly by God Himself. He created us with gifts and abilities so we can express His love to the world. We draw people to Him when we use our gifts to display His love and mighty works to those around us.

> "He creates each of us by Christ Jesus to join him in the work he does, the good work he has gotten ready for us to do, work we had better be doing" (Ephesians 2:10 MSG).

Why Share?

> "It is my pleasure to tell you about the miraculous signs and wonders that the Most High God has performed for me" (Daniel 4:2 NIV).

We all have a history, and thus, we all have a story. If we have a relationship with God, we also have a spiritual testimony. These testimonies are powerful and enlightening to others who are going through similar situations; however, they can only hear them if we share them.

When I was a little girl in Ohio, our church would occasionally have an "open mic" night during which members of the congregation were invited to go up on the stage and share testimonies. I always looked forward to those nights, and decades later, I can still remember some of the testimonies.

One that I remember was told by a "founding mother" of my home church. She told us about the struggles the congregation had in getting the church building built. One specific story she told was about a day during construction when a windstorm threatened to blow down the newly raised walls. The congregation met at the church and worked together to physically hold the walls up until the storm was over.

As interesting as that was, perhaps the most powerful testimony I remember was the one my own grandfather shared. After 50 or more years of dealing with this privately and internally, he finally shared an experience from his 3 1/2 years as a prisoner in a Japanese prison camp in the Philippines during World War II. He told us about a night when he just couldn't take the abuse any longer, and he decided to lie down on the ground and die. While there, he said he distinctly heard God tell him to get up because He was not finished with him yet. Thankfully, my grandfather obeyed or I would not be here, and we would not have my precious grandfather's legacy of God's tender touch during the very worst of times.

While these testimonies are from people who have passed away many years ago, their rich history of hope and survival is still alive. Their testimonies still linger in my mind and hopefully in the memories of others.

We all have a story. To share our stories is to make God's promises, His words, and His works come alive, not only to us but also to those who are listening. If we dare to share them, who knows how many generations of listeners will carry our legacies with them on their own spiritual journeys.

> "Give praise to the Lord, proclaim his name; make known among the nations what he has done" (1 Chronicles 16:8 NIV).

A Ministry of Love

"Be devoted to one another in love. Honor one another above yourselves" (Romans 12:10 NIV).

I recently went to a funeral for Ms. Emma, a dear friend whom I attended church with for many, many years. She was a beautiful woman on the outside, but she was even more beautiful on the inside. She was the shining example of how to be a warm and glowing light to the world.

Ms. Emma always greeted everyone with a smile. No matter how bad she felt or what was going on in her life, she gave us all a smile. She didn't stop there, however; she also freely gave nice, warm hugs. Her hugs were magical in that they seemed to make anything and everything better. After a hug from Ms. Emma, we knew we were loved, and we felt encouraged.

Until her death and her funeral, I don't think we ever realized how powerful her one-on-one, daily ministry was to people. She made each person feel so special individually that we didn't think collectively about how many people she had touched in her lifetime. An excellent example of this effect was the appearance of a grocery store clerk at the funeral. The clerk said he had bagged her groceries every Thursday for many years, and she always talked and listened to him, gave him a hug, and told him that she loved him. He was so affected that he came to her funeral, and he was sobbing so hard he could barely introduce himself to the family.

Ms. Emma's ministry was to make the world better one person at a time as she went about her daily life. She was the warm smile, the listening ear, the loving and sympathetic heart, and the warm and embracing arms of Jesus to everyone. Though she is gone, I know her ministry will continue to live on in the hearts of those she took the opportunity to love. What a wonderful legacy to leave to the world!

"Let your light shine before men in such a way that they may see your good works, and glorify your Father who is in heaven" (Matthew 5:16 NASB).

Preparing To Say Goodbye

ꕔ

"Peace I leave with you; my peace I give you. I do not give to you as the world gives. Do not let your hearts be troubled and do not be afraid" (John 14:27 NIV).

Mr. Gene, a great friend and church family member, was a blessing to everyone he met because God's love was all over him. It overflowed his soul, and he willingly spilled it out warmly upon everyone. When we looked in his eyes, we knew we were loved. In his tender embrace, we felt joy and peace from the tops of our heads to the bottoms of our feet.

When Mr. Gene became ill and entered into his last days, he and his family graciously invited loved ones to visit him to say goodbye. It took me a while, but I finally found the courage to go see him. His eyes lit up when I walked into his room. He hugged me and grabbed my hand to hold it. When he did, I started sobbing, and I couldn't stop. My heart was breaking. I loved him like he was my grandfather, and I didn't want him to go. In typical Mr. Gene fashion, he ended up comforting me when I had visited to comfort him.

Thinking back over that moment, I can empathize with Jesus' disciples as He prepared them for His departure. They did not understand or want to believe He was going, and it deeply hurt them to even think about it. Knowing their feelings, Jesus told them that He was not leaving them alone; He would send a Comforter to help them until He could come back again.

Jesus was referring to the Holy Spirit when He spoke of the Comforter. This name is one of many we have for Him. Other names include Intercessor, Counselor, Helper, Guide, Teacher, Witness, and Revealer of Sin. His names reveal what He does for us. Jesus used the term Comforter because that is who the disciples needed in the difficult days ahead.

I understood how they felt, for I desperately needed God's comfort as I left Mr. Gene for the last time. I didn't need judgment or guidance; I needed reassurance, hope, and love, which is exactly how the Holy

Spirit ministered to me that day and afterward when Mr. Gene passed away. By reminding me and Mr. Gene's loved ones that he was now happy and healthy and living with Jesus in heaven, the Holy Spirit gave us the tremendous comfort and peace we needed, which only He could have provided.

"And I will pray the Father, and he shall give you another Comforter, that he may abide with you forever" (John 14:16 KJV).

Seeing as Jesus Did

~

"Nathanael said to him, 'How do you know me?' Jesus answered, 'Before Philip called you, when you were under the fig tree, I saw you'" (John 1:48 ESV).

When I was little, I was super shy, so I didn't like being the center of attention. It thrilled my heart to get through a day of school without being noticed or singled out by the teacher. I was so timid that I rarely spoke to anyone, and when I did, I spoke so softy people could barely hear me.

Occasionally though, adults would take time to get to know me on a one-on-one basis or in a small group of people, which made me feel less afraid to speak and freer to add my viewpoint to the conversation. These special people were from my church; they were my missions' group, Sunday School, and youth group leaders. They made me feel safe and valued because they took the time to patiently draw me into the group.

Our Lord Jesus was also one of these people. He saw the hidden people who were overlooked or too afraid to be close to him. He saw the small-statured tax collector, Zacchaeus, watching from up in a tree. He saw an ostracized woman drawing water from a public well in the middle of the day. He saw a blind man begging in the street for bread. He saw ten isolated lepers and a bleeding woman with no hope of healing. He saw little children clamoring to be near him. He saw a Roman centurion hungering for His salvation. He saw several local fishermen as leaders for His ministry.

Jesus purposefully sought out people who were at their point of deepest need. He noticed the forgotten, overlooked, and disrespected, and He gave them value. He listened to them, spent time with them, and let them know that they were important to Him.

I, for one, am glad that someone followed His example and saw value in me. By doing so, they changed my life for the better. I pray that we will also have the courage to follow Jesus' example and see others as He did; if we do, God can use us to extend His life-changing love to people who desperately need it.

"Do nothing out of selfish ambition or vain conceit. Rather, in humility value others above yourselves, not looking to your own interests but each of you to the interests of the others" (Philippians 2:3-4 NIV).

The Rich Young Ruler

"As Jesus started on his way, a man ran up to him and fell on his knees before him. 'Good teacher,' he asked, 'what must I do to inherit eternal life?'" (Mark 10:17 NIV).

The passage above is from the account of the rich young ruler, a young man who comes to Jesus seeking eternal life. I have literally heard this story since I was on the church cradle roll, so it is familiar. However, upon reading it again recently, I noticed some important parts of the story for the first time.

First, I noticed when the man approached Jesus, he fell to his knees, and he referred to Jesus as "Good Teacher." When I was a child, I pictured him dressed in a royal robe, flippantly asking Jesus this question because he wanted to trap him or to follow the crowd. The fact that he fell to his knees and addressed Jesus personally revealed to me that he had been an active and devoted follower of Jesus.

Second, I noticed the statement "Jesus looked at him and loved him" (Mark 10:21 NIV). I had only remembered the second half of that verse when Jesus tells him that he lacked charity because he held on to possessions too tightly. I had always thought Jesus was stern with him until I read this verse and realized that Jesus corrected the young man tenderly with mercy and love. This look of love was so powerful it was included in scripture.

I believe when we get to heaven, Jesus will also look at us with love when He welcomes us into His kingdom. I know I will melt into a puddle at His feet, and I am sure I will not be the only one. For to be loved so wholly and unconditionally by Someone who knows everything about us must be extremely overwhelming. It is a feeling our souls have longed for our entire lives. I can't imagine being able to bear it without feeling compelled to worship Him in love and gratitude. It must be humbling and wonderful to be in His presence, completely covered in His love.

> "Give thanks to the God of heaven. *His love endures forever*" (Psalm 136:26 NIV).

Our Father's Love

> "'And I will be a father to you, and you shall be sons and daughters to me,' says the Lord Almighty" (2 Corinthians 6:18 ESV).

I noticed a picture in the newspaper of a young girl I know playing basketball for her local high school. I was glad to see her doing well and being recognized for her hard work. Then I looked behind her and saw her dad sitting in the stands. He was beaming so brightly with pride and love that I would have guessed he was her dad even if I didn't know them.

As I looked at the picture, I thought about our relationship with God. I wondered if our Heavenly Father looks at us with such emotion. Looking to Jesus as our God-on-earth, I found my answer. Jesus expressed tenderness toward the children, sadness over the death of Lazarus, and anger toward the moneychangers in the temple. He felt sympathy for those who needed His touch and disappointment for those who rejected Him. So God obviously watches us intently and is emotionally involved in our lives. I imagine He celebrates when we do something well for Him, mourns when we mourn, and is disappointed when we reject Him.

He loves us with strong emotion as does a good father. As His beloved children, we should feel compelled to express our love back to Him. Our dedication to Him should be evident and our gratitude well-known. We should strive to live in a way that pleases Him so He is proud of us. He is a good Father, and He truly deserves our loyalty and sincere adoration.

"See what great love the Father has lavished on us, that we should be called children of God! And that is what we are! The reason the world does not know us is that it did not know him" (1 John 3:1 NIV).

He Knows Our Intentions

"[W]ould not God have discovered it, since he knows the secrets of the heart?" (Psalm 44:21 NIV).

When I was probably around three years old, I decided I was going to help my mom clean up, or maybe even redecorate, the living room. I worked hard for several minutes moving stuff around and putting like-items together. Then I proudly called my mom in to look at it, and I can still feel the shock of seeing my mom's horrified face as she looked over what I had done. Apparently in my little-kid efforts to clean up and put things in order, I had left the living room in total disarray.

Even though my mom could not see or understand my intentions nor could I explain them to her, God knew what they were then and knows what they are now. He is not limited with human eyes and understanding. He sees straight through our hearts to our attitudes and our true intentions. The Bible says in Jeremiah 17:10 that the Lord rewards us based on what He finds while searching our hearts and minds. Matthew 6:2 warns us that when we minister with a self-serving attitude, whatever reward we receive on earth is all the reward we will ever receive.

It can be both comforting and frightening to know that God sees our motives; however, that knowledge can inspire us to closely examine our hearts. Going through the process of clearing out clutter and examining our true intentions can help us grow closer to God. Then, hopefully, as a result, we will see a real difference in our effectiveness as we serve Him and serve others in His name.

"Above all else, guard your heart, for everything you do flows from it" (Proverbs 4:23 NIV).

Never Alone

"Pour out all your worries and stress upon him *and leave them there*, for he always tenderly cares for you" (1 Peter 5:7 TPT).

When I went outside this morning, my lungs and my throat burned as they filled with smoke and cried out for fresh mountain air. It was then that I was reminded of the horrible wildfires going on in the mountains all around us. I thought about the firefighters and neighbors who are out in it and how hard it must be for them to breathe.

My current situation reminded me of a time when I was a college student in Kentucky and a wildfire burned on a mountain near us. Ash fell from the sky like snow, and smoke thickly filled the air. Another day in college, I remember worrying about the river flooding and covering the only bridge leading out of town. I'll never forget truthfully telling my mother that I would be home, "Lord willing, and the creek don't rise."

We face changing weather and the resulting circumstances daily, areas over which we have no control. Science has studied weather for years and years, yet meteorologists cannot always predict it correctly. Even when they do, we can do nothing to change it: we are literally at its mercy. We have to plan around it and prepare for it the best we can.

No matter what weather or tragedy comes our way, we are not without hope, however. We are reminded in the Bible that God is bigger than the weather and our circumstances. We pray for rain to put out the wildfires, but if we don't get it, He promises to be with us as we go through the fire. No matter what circumstance in which we find ourselves—even if we pass from this life into the next—we can be sure that we will never be alone.

> "But now the Lord who created you, O Israel, says: Don't be afraid, for I have ransomed you; I have called you by name; you are mine. When you go through deep waters and great trouble, I will be with you. When you go through rivers of difficulty, you will not drown! When you walk through the fire of oppression, you will not be burned up—the flames will not consume you" (Isaiah 43:1-2 TLB).

The Inspirational Birdsong

$\heartsuit$

"The flowers are springing up, the season of singing birds
has come, and the cooing of turtledoves fills the air"
(Song of Solomon 2:12 NLT).

This morning when I arrived at my work church, I went into the
sanctuary to start working on the presentation slides for Sunday's
worship service. The sanctuary was quiet, empty, and dark, which is
usual for a weekday morning.

I made my way up to the balcony, turned on the computer, and
waited for it to load. As I sat there in the dark sanctuary, I was blessed to
hear a bird singing from somewhere outside the building. The beautiful
song seemed to fill the entire empty sanctuary with a volume much
bigger than the tiny bird seemed capable of making. It was so beautiful
and calming that I felt compelled to sit still and listen. I felt in my spirit
that this bird was worshipping its Creator with its whole heart, and
ironically, its song filled a large, empty sanctuary, a place dedicated to
worshipping God.

God inspired this little bird's song, and the bird gratefully sang
its heart out to bless God. Then God made its song a concert for one
and used it to inspire these words. If we think about God's inspiration,
we'll realize its power. We would simply be lumps of clay without God's
inspirational breath. The Bible would be an ordinary book but for
God giving His writers His words to record on pages and empowering
the words to touch lives for centuries. God then inspires preachers,
empowering them to make the ancient scripture's truth applicable to
our everyday, modern lives.

This tiny bird with the big sound shared a powerful lesson today.
God gives us breath and passion to do something beautiful for Him,
and when we do, He will use our obedience to do astonishing things for
His kingdom. In the process, we will be blessed in the task, God will be
blessed in our obedience, and those who witness or receive benefit from
what we do will be blessed as well.

"God has given each of you a gift from his great variety of spiritual gifts. Use them well to serve one another. Do you have the gift of speaking? Then speak as though God himself were speaking through you. Do you have the gift of helping others? Do it with all the strength and energy that God supplies. Then everything you do will bring glory to God through Jesus Christ. All glory and power to him forever and ever! Amen" (1 Peter 4:10-11 NLT).

The Sweet Aroma of Jesus

"Then Mary took about a pint of pure nard, an expensive perfume; she poured it on Jesus' feet and wiped his feet with her hair. And the house was filled with the fragrance of the perfume" (John 12:3 NIV).

Our sense of smell is powerful, allowing fragrances to fill our minds and enhance our life experiences. It helps us to discern flavor on our tongues. It warns us if something is fresh or spoiled or if an imminent danger is nearby, such as smoky fire, a fuel leak, or a poisonous mold growth. Scents also evoke powerful memories and emotions. The smell of the ocean can remind us of a beach vacation, the smell of new crayons and plastic notebooks can remind us of school, and certain perfumes can remind us of loved ones.

Another facet of scents is that they can permeate the air of a space. The sweet aroma of a Thanksgiving meal cooking can make everyone in the house hungry. The sickening odor of trash, mothballs, or skunk can force people to leave the area. Unfortunately, these smells can even attach to our clothing and hair and be inadvertently shared with others wherever we go.

The Bible tells us that we are to be the aroma of Christ to the world. Applying this metaphor to the information above, we are to carry

Him with us and share His love everywhere we go. Our attitudes, our demeanor, our words, and our actions should all attract people to Jesus. When we enter or leave a group, others should notice because feelings of peace and love should come and go with us. When people remember us, they should automatically think of positive qualities such as love and kindness, which we exhibited because Christ was alive through us.

In order for Mary to be able to anoint Jesus with the expensive perfume, as mentioned in the verse above, she first had to open the bottle. Likewise, if we are to spread the aroma of Christ, we have to open ourselves up to do so. God is able to spread His lovely aroma through us by way of the Holy Spirit, who carries it from our hearts to the hearts of people around us. Many lives can be changed, including our own, but first, we have to yield ourselves to God as vessels from which He can pour out His love.

> "Through our yielded lives he spreads the fragrance of the knowledge of God everywhere we go. We have become the unmistakable aroma *of the victory* of the Anointed One to God—a perfume of life to those being saved and the odor of death to those who are perishing" (2 Corinthians 2:14b-15 TPT).

Fighting the Cravings

> "Enter through the narrow gate. For wide is the gate and broad is the road that leads to destruction, and many enter through it. But small is the gate and narrow the road that leads to life, and only a few find it" (Matthew 7:13-14 NIV).

I made a resolution once to try a gluten-free diet. I have chronic joint pain, and I had heard that eating gluten caused swelling and pain in those areas. Eliminating gluten was definitely not easy, and I was not always successful in my plan.

One day in the midst of my diet, I had a real craving for a certain fast food of no nutritional value, a food which I had been avoiding for a year. When I got to the restaurant, however, there was a double line of cars backed up all the way around the building. To make matters worse, people who had parked and eaten inside were now trying to back out through the drive-thru lines to leave, but the drivers in line wouldn't let them out. The line was three cars deep in some places, a deadlocked traffic jam.

Then the verse above popped in my mind. I thought about all of these people, including me, who were at that moment clamoring for food that was not good for us and was apparently addicting. It's like we are racing to an early death and shoving others to get there first.

With this realization, my craving went away immediately, and I decided to make something healthier at home. The experience changed me, however, because I now had a vivid picture of how deceptive and destructive the wide paths of life can be and how gullibly we join the crowd walking down them. This situation made it even more evident to me that protecting our spiritual hearts is as important as protecting our physical hearts. Thus, putting on our God-given armor every day is truly necessary for our protection while we are living in this world.

> "Finally, be strong in the Lord and in his mighty power. Put on the full armor of God, so that you can take your stand against the devil's schemes" (Ephesians 6:10-11 NIV).

Bigger Than Our Trials

♡

"No test or temptation that comes your way is beyond the course of what others have had to face. All you need to remember is that God will never let you down; he'll never let you be pushed past your limit; he'll always be there to help you come through it" (1 Corinthians 10:13 MSG).

One of the phrases that is often used when we are feeling overwhelmed is "God won't give me more than I can handle." That, however, is only the first part of 1 Corinthians 10:13. The above verse goes on to say that when we can't handle our trials, God will help us through them. For if we could handle everything on our own, we would never see our need for God. Our helplessness reveals our weakness and compels us to seek God's help.

In my own experience, when my husband received a stage four brain cancer diagnosis, we were on our knees praying, and we were reading the Bible all the time. We knew this situation was way beyond our human ability. We were forced to make life and death decisions about things we knew little or nothing about. We knew that if we were to get through this trial, God had to lead us and walk beside us all the way.

For my husband, his eventual way out of his pain and suffering was death, a way of escape God provided for him through Jesus, who died for us many years ago. My way of escape was similar in that his death alleviated a lot of my daily pain and suffering; however, it ushered in brand new types of trials: grief, widowhood, and single motherhood. God didn't let go of me though. He continued to help me by providing the resources and supportive people that I needed when I needed them.

Our trials are actually opportunities to get to know and work with the Almighty God. He is bigger and stronger than whatever we face, yet He is also the most tender, gracious, merciful, and loving friend we could ever have. We can trust and follow Him because He cares so much about us.

"Let the morning bring me word of your unfailing love, for I have put my trust in you. Show me the way I should go, for to you I entrust my life" (Psalm 143:8 NIV).

Being Finished

"When he had received the drink, Jesus said, 'It is finished.' With that, he bowed his head and gave up his spirit" (John 19:30 NIV).

There is nothing quite like the feelings that come with finally being able to say, "I'm finished." We often say it with a sigh of relief because we've completed a challenging task. We've finally reached the point when we can step back and admire all that we've worked so long and hard to accomplish.

When Jesus exhaled, "It is finished," His words had a powerful and everlasting impact. It meant that He had satisfied our death penalty so we could live eternally with Him, and it meant that He successfully bridged the gap separating sinful us from our Most Holy God. Most of all, it emphasized the fact that Jesus chose to endure suffering unto death because He loves us.

Jesus' death and resurrection completed His mission to bring salvation to the world. However, it wasn't just an end: it was a beginning. It ushered in a new era of grace and open communication between us and God. Jesus opened the door for the Holy Spirit to come and dwell within us so now we can enjoy a close, personal relationship with our loving Heavenly Father. We now live with the hope and promise of an eternal life spent in Heaven with Him because Jesus finished His mission to save us.

"Jesus said to her, 'I am the resurrection and the life. The one who believes in me will live, even though they die;

and whoever lives by believing in me will never die. Do you believe this?'" (John 11:25-26 NIV).

Cleaning Up Easter

"He is not here, he has risen! Remember how he told you, while he was still with you in Galilee: 'The Son of Man must be delivered over to the hands of sinners, be crucified and on the third day be raised again'" (Luke 24:6-7 NIV).

Another Easter has come and gone. All of the cute little Easter outfits, no longer new, are cast aside to be hung up or washed. The Easter baskets have been rifled through and the candy consumed by excited little children. The Easter meal leftovers are stashed away in the fridge to enjoy later. This year's Easter has been officially crossed off the calendar and is now only found in memories and photographs.

We put away the adornments of Easter, but that shouldn't be the case for Christ and His resurrection. Without the resurrection, we would have never known the significance of Jesus' death. He would have gone down in history as another revolutionary who had been killed. However, because He rose to live again, we know that He was exactly who He said He was. It is the foundation of our faith in Him.

As did the women who heard the words in the verse above, we have a choice to make regarding our remembrance of Jesus' resurrection. We can put it in the past, file it away for next Easter, and not let it affect us, or we can choose to carry it forward into our day-to-day life. Only because believers decided to share this resurrection news with us have we been given the opportunity to have eternal life; therefore, it is now up to our generation to share it with others. If we refuse, many people, both present and future, may be lost forever in their sins.

"So go and make followers of all people in the world. Baptize them in the name of the Father and the Son and the Holy Spirit. Teach them to obey everything that I have told you to do. You can be sure that I will be with you always. I will continue with you until the end of time" (Matthew 28:19-20 ERV).

Comforting Coats

"Now Israel loved Joseph more than any other of his sons, because he was the son of his old age. And he made him a robe of many colors" (Genesis 37:3 ESV).

It's almost time for trick-or-treating—the time kids look forward to and school teachers dread. Even though I did not love candy as a child, I looked forward to trick-or-treating. I usually dressed as Cinderella, which included a thin, plastic, printed dress worn over my clothes and a plastic mask with nose and mouth holes through which I struggled to breathe. If I think about it, I can still smell that plastic mask as it pressed up against my nose.

I knew I was going to face a battle with my mother every year because she would insist that I wear a coat over my costume. I always argued that no one could see my costume if I wore a coat over it. Even at that age, I didn't see the point of the costume if I had to cover it up. Nevertheless, my mom always won even in the mild Texas Octobers. I knew deep in my heart that she was right and that she was trying to keep me warm and healthy because she loved me.

Just as we all wear many "hats" in life, we also wear many coats, covering ourselves with the one thing that makes us feel secure, comfortable, and insulated. For many years, I wore a "grief coat" which surrounded me in misery but in which I had become comfortable. When

I became aware of the fact that I was living comfortably in this coat of misery, I began the hard work of therapy to remove it.

Other symbolic coats we can wear include fear, sadness, status, vocation, relationships, and even religion. Whatever keeps us comfortable yet separated and protected from our true feelings can be a coat. Unfortunately, these coats can also keep us separated from God and from the best He has planned for our lives. An examination and sacrifice of our self-made, insulated coat may be in order so that we can be freely adorned with the garment of grace that God has lovingly made for us.

> "But his father said to the servants, 'Quick! Bring the finest robe in the house and put it on him. Get a ring for his finger and sandals for his feet. And kill the calf we have been fattening. We must celebrate with a feast, for this son of mine was dead and has now returned to life. He was lost, but now he is found.' So the party began" (Luke 15:22-24 NLT).

"Get To" versus "Have To"

> "A joyful heart is good medicine, but a crushed spirit dries up the bones" (Proverbs 17:22 ESV).

The week before Thanksgiving is usually a busy week in a church office. There is always a lot of work to do and only three working days to do it in. It's exhausting work yet exciting at the same time, for at the end of those three working days is Thanksgiving.

Sitting at my desk, I often hear a variety of Thanksgiving plans. Some people express excitement about having family and friends come in to visit and share Thanksgiving with them. Others indicate that they are not looking forward to spending time with extended family or about fixing a Thanksgiving meal.

I have especially noticed two often-used phrases which indicate someone's true feelings about a situation. These phrases are "get to" and "have to." If office visitors say they "get to" go to a Thanksgiving dinner, we sense an excitement about it. However, if they say they "have to," we get the sense they are being forced to do something against their will.

In thinking about these phrases, I wondered if they also apply spiritually. How many times have we said we "have to" go to church, read our Bible, pray, tithe, spend time in Bible study and fellowship, etc.? What does the use of this promise say about us?

How different would it be to say we "get to" spend time talking with God, "get to" go to church and worship, "get to" fellowship with God's people, "get to" serve in the nursery or in the kitchen, or "get to" give food to a family who needs help? Changing one simple word means we now look forward to these activities, resulting in a changed mindset on the entire effort.

I can't speak for God, but I venture to guess that He would take a "We get to" over a "We have to" from us any day. Wouldn't we all?

> "O God, You are my God; earnestly I seek You; my soul thirsts for You; my flesh faints for You, as in a dry and weary land where there is no water" (Psalm 63:1 ESV)

Expecting His Arrival

> "So the Lord himself will give you this sign: A virgin will become pregnant and give birth to a son, and she will name him Immanuel [God Is With Us]" (Isaiah 7:14 GW).

I think the question that gets asked most frequently in December is "Are you ready for Christmas?" I venture to guess that, more often than not, the answer is "no." Unfortunately, even if we want it here earlier or later, Christmas always comes on December 25th whether we are ready or not.

At the first Christmas, many people were obviously not ready for the birth of Jesus either. We only know of a few who received a word from God and believed and accepted in faith: Mary, Joseph, and Elizabeth (Mary's cousin) expected His birth; the wise men anticipated His arrival and traveled a long distance to meet Him; at Jesus' presentation at the temple, Anna and Simeon were overjoyed when they met him and recognized him as the Messiah they had been waiting for.

This small band of people, ranging from kings to carpenters, paled in comparison to the rest of civilization who were not ready for Him. Jewish religious leaders certainly did not expect the Messiah to arrive as a baby born to a common woman, and they were instrumental in steering most of the nation of Israel away from believing as well. King Herod wanted to kill Him because the magi referred to Him as a future king, which threatened Herod's reign. For whatever reason, most of the people who walked around in their daily lives next to God in human form did not recognize Him as such.

Before we criticize, we need to remember that if we are Christians, we have the Holy Spirit of God inside of us. Just think of all the places we have taken Him, the things we have shown Him through our eyes, the thoughts we have thought in His presence, and the words we have said or not said—it is truly humbling to consider. We talk about getting ourselves ready for Jesus' second coming and we should, but we need to also remember that the Holy Spirit is already here inside us. He is our God-on-earth as Jesus once was and will be again. Therefore, we should live our lives as if God is always with us because He *is* always with us.

> "And be sure of this: I am with you always, even to the end of the age" (Matthew 28:20b NLT).

A Different Kind of Broken

"The Lord is close to the brokenhearted and saves those who are crushed in spirit" (Psalm 34:18 NIV)

In one of my Bible study groups, we discussed the idea of praying for a compassionate heart. In my opinion, that is a bold prayer because in order to have a compassionate heart, we have to let God break it for something. We have to make ourselves vulnerable to Him.

If you have ever had your heart thoroughly broken, you know it is not something to look forward to or something you necessarily want to happen again. When we are hurt, it is our human tendency to recoil and put a wall of protection around ourselves. Doing so may be good for a time in order to heal, but too long and we can become so afraid and so guarded that we shut ourselves off from life and love.

I am currently emerging from a long season of repeated brokenness, and so until now, the thought of allowing God to break me has been a most frightening idea. However, by God's grace, I am discovering that His brokenness is different than what I am used to experiencing. It is not His goal to destroy us but to rebuild and reshape us into something better. As we grow and change with time and experience, God wants to give us new passions and purposes so that our lives are meaningful to us and useful to Him. We have to choose to join Him in that work by removing our walls and trusting in His process. If we do, He will make our hearts new and open to fresh passions and great joy, and He will turn our brokenness into praise.

"You turned my wailing into dancing: you removed my sackcloth and clothed me with joy, that my heart may sing your praises and not be silent. Lord my God, I will praise you forever" (Psalm 30:11-12 NIV).

Wrestling in Prayer

♡

"Epaphras, who is one of you and a servant of Christ Jesus, sends greetings. He is always wrestling in prayer for you, that you may stand firm in all the will of God, mature and fully assured" (Colossians 4:12 NIV).

As I read this verse, I was struck with the wording "wrestled in prayer for you." It seemed an odd way of describing Epaphras' prayer life. When I think of the word "wrestling," I think back to the heyday of TV wrestling on Saturday nights. In those contexts, I would not think to put the words "wrestling" and "prayer" together.

However, when I think about it, the combination makes sense. A person who is earnestly praying is engaging in a battle of the wills, such as two people engaged in a wrestling match. We see this idea played out in Jesus's life as He prayed in the Garden of Gethsemane, "Not My will, but Thine be done" (Luke 22:42). He struggled so hard that His sweat was like drops of blood (Luke 22:44).

Epaphras' fervent and passionate prayers clearly impressed Paul, so much so that Paul felt compelled to mention them to his readers as a word of encouragement. We would all do well to have such a prayer warrior friend; actually, we would all do well to become such a prayer warrior.

"Admit your faults to one another and pray for each other so that you may be healed. The earnest prayer of a righteous man has great power and wonderful results" (James 5:16 TLB).

The God Who Answers Prayers

♡

"Then you will call on me and come and pray to me, and I will listen to you" (Jeremiah 29:12 NIV).

Prayer is one of the most personal ways that we communicate with God. There are many ways to pray, and we do not all pray in the same way. Some of us may pray at a certain time every day, and others may pray a little bit throughout the day. Others may pray only when they are knee deep in dead fish in the belly of a whale (Jonah 2:1) and others when they are just shopping for shoes. Regardless of your style of prayer and how trivial or critical the situation, we can be sure that our prayers are heard and answered.

When I think how we pray, I think of children making requests of their parents. Some do so with whining, crying, and manipulation to try to get what they want. Others try to bargain and make promises in exchange for getting their desires. Still others ask for something that is unsafe, and their parents have to deny them because they can see dangers their children cannot see. But if children ask for something that is safe, appropriate, and well-deserved, then often the parents will give them what they ask if at all possible.

God also knows the truth of what we need versus what we think we need. He measures our maturity and our trustworthiness, deciding what is best for us and choosing whether to answer now or when we are ready. He might make us wait until He can give us an answer that is better than what we prayed for, hoped for, or even dreamed possible. He may even surprise us by answering prayers we have not yet prayed.

Whether we get exactly what we ask for or not, prayer is our way to communicate with our Father. Frequent communication with God makes our personal relationship with Him stronger. The stronger our relationship and the closer we are to Him, the easier it will be for us to discern the subtle work He is doing in our lives.

"I will answer them before they even call to me. While they are still talking about their needs, I will go ahead and answer their prayers!" (Isaiah 65:24 NLT).

Pray Believing and Never Stop

$\heartsuit$

"So Peter was kept in prison, but the church was earnestly praying to God for him (Acts. 12:5 NIV).

Acts 12 contains one of my favorite Bible stories about prayer. At the beginning of the chapter, we find Peter in prison, chained between two guards, waiting to go on trial the next day. Suddenly an angel appears and instantly the chains fall off. The angel then leads Peter out of the prison and through the city gates. Peter first thinks he is dreaming, but after coming to himself outside the city gates, he soon knows that it actually happened.

Peter flees to the home of John Mark's mother, Mary, who's hosting a church prayer meeting to pray for Peter. He knocks on the door, and Rhoda, a servant girl, goes to answer it. When she hears Peter's voice on the other side of the door, she gets so excited that she runs and tells everyone without letting him in first. The people there, although earnestly praying for his freedom, do not believe Rhoda and argue with her. Peter continues to knock, and, eventually, they answer the door and see that he really is standing there. Peter explains to them how the angel freed him, and he asks them to spread the news of his freedom to other believers. Then he leaves for another place.

The Bible story is one of my favorites because it plays out almost like a TV sitcom; however, the lesson that this story teaches is most serious. The people earnestly prayed for God to save Peter, but apparently, they didn't expect God to answer their prayers or to answer in that way. Of course, it was an unusual and unexpected answer, but even when presented with the truth, they didn't believe it, and in fact, they argued against it. The story begs the question, do we really pray believing or expecting God to answer? Do we watch for an answer and recognize it when it comes? As the proverbial story of old asks, do we come to a prayer meeting to pray for rain but leave our umbrellas at home? I wonder how much richer our prayer life and our relationship with God would be if we prayed with faith and expectation that He is listening to us and working out an answer to our prayer.

> "But as for me, I watch in hope for the Lord, I wait for God my Savior; my God will hear me" (Micah 7:7 NIV).

A Painful Pinky

> "Stay alert! Watch out for your great enemy, the devil. He prowls around like a roaring lion, looking for someone to devour" (1 Peter 5:8 NLT).

I have developed arthritis in the top joint of my left pinky finger recently. While I have lived with arthritis pain in my knees and hips for several years, the pain of this tiny finger has been particularly noticeable. Simple tasks such as stacking and washing dishes, folding clothes, searching for an item in my purse, putting on makeup, lifting weights, and shelving books have all become painful for me. Since it is the pinky of my dominant hand, I am sure there are more painful discoveries ahead of me.

As a writer and administrative assistant, I spend most of my time typing, and thus my sore pinky has seriously interfered with my skills. I have found it especially painful to reach up and type an exclamation point, which I often use in my writing to express joy and excitement. So basically, I am faced with a choice: I can stop using the exclamation point; I can continue to use it and suffer the pain; or I can learn to use another finger to access it. In essence, I was deciding whether I would allow the pain to steal the joy I feel when I write as well as the joy I express in my writing.

The Bible says that the devil prowls around looking for someone to devour. I am sure he would love to stop me from sharing God's love in my writing. He knows that God's joy is powerful; it motivates Christians to share the salvation message, and it attracts non-Christians to listen to it.

Our enemy is clever, but he is no match for the power of God. No matter how hard he tries, he can never completely eradicate joy from our lives because it comes from God who has an endless supply. God shares it with us freely because He finds *His* joy in blessing His children.

> "Now may God, the inspiration and fountain of hope, fill you to overflowing with uncontainable joy and perfect peace as you trust in him. And may the power of the Holy Spirit continually surround your life with his super-abundance until you radiate with hope!" (Romans 15:13 TPT).

Our Own Devices

> "But my people would not listen to me; Israel would not submit to me. So I gave them over to their stubborn hearts to follow their own devices" (Psalm 81:11-12 NIV).

God brought this verse to my mind, and as I recited it in my head, I became stuck on the word "devices." When the scholars originally used this word in the Bible, they defined it as schemes, plots, plans, and tactics. However, in today's society, what first comes to mind when reading or hearing the word "devices" are cell phones, computers, personal fitness devices, TV's, and other such personal technology.

In studying this word, I found it fascinating to discover that our definition of devices is still appropriate for this verse. If we follow our devices too closely, we shut out the voice of God. Rather than wait for God to reveal His will, we'd rather access the opinions of others immediately. Our minds are constantly filled with news and opinions via the internet and television broadcasts. We can also be tempted to access ungodly sites that contain content often viewed in private which would humiliate us in public. With a wide-range of information bombarding us all day, every day, it is difficult to avoid being influenced by worldly opinions and convictions.

Our modern devices are not just used for evil though. Today more people than ever have access to the Bible via computer and phone applications. People are reading their Bibles more often and can reference it instantly when sharing the gospel with people. Prayer requests can be shared globally, calling multitudes of people to pray over a single need. We can rejoice with millions when we learn of a great movement of revival or ministry anywhere in the world. On a personal level, we can encourage and support our friends and family at almost any time from any place.

In today's context, being left to our own devices can be good or bad, depending on what our devices are used for and to whom we are listening. We have to remain hyper vigilant to make sure we don't allow devices to take the place of God in our hearts. He wants and deserves to be first in our lives every day.

> "Those who live according to the flesh have their minds set on what the flesh desires; but those who live in accordance with the Spirit have their minds set on what the Spirit desires" (Romans 8:5 NIV).

An Undo Button

♡

"Lord, I know that people's lives are not their own; it is not for them to direct their steps" (Jeremiah 10:23 NIV).

I believe that one of the best inventions in the development of computer programming is the "undo" button. I have worked with several word-processing programs, each of them different and requiring training and practice to learn. If it wasn't for that "undo" button, I would have lost many documents.

Wouldn't it be nice if life had an undo button? If we say something or do something we shouldn't, we could just hit that undo button and try again. When a decision doesn't turn out the way we want, we could hit the undo button until it is comes out right. I suspect this button would be worn out from frequent use.

The problem with this idea though is that it would put us in the driver's seat. God did not give us an undo option, probably because we couldn't handle it. Instead of moving forward or facing the outcomes of our mistakes, we would rewind our way through life, forcing it to go our way.

Rather than an undo option, He gave us advice on how to get along with others and how to reconcile our differences. It takes effort and humility to fix the aftermath of mistakes and disagreements, but if God is in the hearts on both sides, lessons can be learned, and wisdom can be gleaned. These experiences can then be used as steps toward to a better relationship.

"Finally, all of you should be of one mind. Sympathize with each other. Love each other as brothers and sisters. Be tenderhearted, and keep a humble attitude" (1 Peter 3:8 NLT).

One Step at a Time

♡

"I will instruct you and teach you in the way you should go; I will counsel you with my loving eye on you" (Psalm 32:8 NIV).

Back in the '80s, computers were just becoming accessible to the public. I remember taking a computer class in high school on a TRS-80 computer, otherwise known by the techno-geeks of the time as "trash 80s." There were four or five computers for the whole class, and they served the entire school.

My class was not anything like a computer class today. There was no software to do word processing or spreadsheets, and there was no internet. Basically, we would write pages of programming to get the computer to do something simple such as write our initials on the screen or draw the figure of a smiley face. This programming was done in equations and flowcharts. Flowcharts were made up of shapes, such as squares and triangles, indicating directions and choices, such as "if, then," start, and finish, among others, and we had to be careful not to lead the computer to think in endless circles.

I am a process-thinker, so I loved this class and classes like geometry. The lessons learned then are still valuable to me because I learned how to think through things one step at a time. I, furthermore, learned each choice had a consequence which would lead me in either the right or the wrong direction.

Now that I am an adult who has lived through the consequences of my wrong choices and the wrong choices of others, I am not always so sure of my next step. Life is certainly no flowchart or rigid math problem. We are bombarded with choices and information, and the internet is quickly replacing the Bible as our world's standard for living.

Rather than relying on the internet, we must rely on God for discernment and for guidance. He is personally involved in our lives, and He knows what is best for us. As our Creator, He also knows that divulging too much information about our futures could easily overwhelm and paralyze us. He chooses, therefore, to walk through life with us and reveal directions to us one or two steps at a time. We have to trust Him enough to follow Him faithfully wherever He leads us.

> "The Lord makes firm the steps of the one who delights in him; though he may stumble, he will not fall, for the Lord upholds him with his hand" (Psalm 37:23-24 NIV).

Turning Back

> "All day long I have held out my hands to an obstinate people, who walk in ways not good, pursuing their own imaginations—a people who continually provoke me to my very face" (Isaiah 65:2-3a NIV).

One Friday morning when I arrived at my work church, I decided to get a jump on the day by powering up the sanctuary computer right away so I could start working on the service slides for Sunday. I entered the front door of the sanctuary and began walking down the aisle toward the balcony stairs at the back of the room. About halfway there, an uneasy feeling suddenly came over me, and I felt as if I had turned my back on God and was purposefully walking away from Him. The further I walked away from the altar, the stronger I felt the urge to turn back. Then a strong sense of guilt and shame washed over me, and I finally decided to turn back to the altar, and as I turned around, I heard God speak an explanation within my spirit.

I understood that God was illustrating what it is like to reject Him. The experience was shameful and not pleasant, and I am sure it was not supposed to be. The push and pull I felt represented the internal struggle between wanting to reconcile with God and wanting to walk away from Him.

No matter how far away we try to go, we will never be able to escape the grasp of God's love. Although His love is a just and holy love, it is tempered with grace, mercy, and forgiveness. God will never stop drawing us to Him or waiting for us to turn back, and when we finally do, He will meet us at the altar and fully embrace us with His love.

"But while he was still a long way off, his father saw him and was filled with compassion for him; he ran to his son, threw his arms around him and kissed him. The son said to him, 'Father, I have sinned against heaven and against you. I am no longer worthy to be called your son.' But the father said to his servants, '. . . Let's have a feast and celebrate. For this son of mine was dead and is alive again; he was lost and is found.' So they began to celebrate" (Luke 15:20-24 NIV).

Humane or Human

"When your lives bear abundant fruit, you demonstrate that you are my mature disciples who glorify my Father!" (John 15:8 TPT).

I have a dear friend who is transitioning at her job from one office to another within the same organization. She shared with me and a mutual friend that during her last staff meeting with her former office coworkers, her boss told her that he would miss her humanity around the office. She didn't understand what he meant by that comment, so she asked for our thoughts on it. We decided to look up the definition online and discovered that in this context, her boss was referencing the word "humane," which meant she was compassionate, benevolent, kind, considerate, and gentle toward others.

This word is a perfect description of her. In fact, her picture should be placed in the dictionary beside the definition as a chief example.

What is ironic, however, is that these qualities are not shared out of her humanity; instead, they are the fruits of the Holy Spirit who lives within her. They are the outward evidence of her inward, beautiful, close, and personal relationship with God.

From this example, we can see how our actions and attitudes reflect our hearts. People notice when we live in close communion with God because our actions and words reflect His love. On the other hand, when we profess to be Christians and do not live the lifestyle, we present an unfavorable impression of God and may drive people away from Him. Therefore, we should treat people with kindness, respect, courtesy, and love as Jesus did so they can see Jesus in us. In so doing, we will become noticeably more humane and less human.

> "Be ready to speak up and tell anyone who asks why you're living the way you are, and always with the utmost courtesy" (1 Peter 3:15b MSG).

The Woman Known as My Sister

> "So go ahead and give her the credit that is due, for she has become a radiant woman, and all her loving works of righteousness deserve to be admired at the gateways of every city!" (Proverbs 31:31 TPT).

A couple of months ago, I enjoyed a nice visit with my family in Ohio. While my visits usually coincide with holidays, this time, there were no holiday events to plan visits around. So we were able to spend some good quality time together.

I especially look forward to staying with my sister when I travel there because I love being near her. That hasn't always been the case, however, for I annoyed her as the bossy older sister, and she pestered me as the baby. We were pretty much inseparable as young girls whether we liked it or not—even when we tried to knock the living daylights out of each other. We then went in separate directions when we grew up, started our families, and sought our niche in the world. In recent years, however, we seem to have grown close again.

This particular visit turned out to be a unique experience for me because God took the opportunity to show my sister to me in a whole new light. He opened my eyes to her kind and loving nature, strong intelligence, hilarious and quick wit, deep friendships, creative nature, and passionate love for God and family. I saw her God-given talent for teaching preschoolers, her passion to prepare them to be successful in school, and her drive to instill them with healthy emotional control, spiritual insight, and educational curiosity. I, furthermore, saw her sweet, tender, empathetic heart and the subtle ways she points others to the throne of God's grace to find their value, help, and salvation. I was touched and blessed to discover this wonderful woman I have known only as my sister.

Through this experience, God took me past the pigeon-holes where society puts people and challenged me to try to see people as He sees them—to look beyond personas, labels, and relationships, to see hearts and potential. For instance, God saw a shepherd boy as a king. Jesus saw fishermen as preachers, tax collectors as disciples, broken women as strong and valuable ministry partners, pious religious leaders as misguided law students, and enemies as friends. Since God sees us with potential, we are not forever stuck in our mistakes or our plights in this world. He gives us new self-worth and a greater hope for a better future. Better still, God provides us with courage, power, and passion to go beyond our self-imposed limitations. He empowers us to do amazing works for His kingdom, and when we trust His vision, He can use us in astounding ways.

> "But those who trust in the Lord will find new strength. They will soar high on wings like eagles. They will run and not grow weary. They will walk and not faint." (Isaiah 40:31 NLT).

Being Homeless

𝕯

"Feed the hungry, and help those in trouble. Then your light will shine out from the darkness, and the darkness around you will be as bright as noon" (Isaiah 58:10 NLT).

A few nights a year, I spend the evening at church hosting families in the Family Promise program, a program which provides temporary housing to homeless families who have children. The families rotate weeks staying overnight in participating churches. Each church hosts the families and provides meals for them. Other church congregations partner with host churches to help with hosting and meals.

Last week was my church's week to host families, and I was scheduled to host on Friday night. In my experience, Friday nights are usually tough because everyone (both hosts and parents) are tired and the kids are often bored and irritable. A former social worker once told me that being poor and homeless is stressful and corralling one's children in someone else's place is difficult. I can only imagine what that is like week after week. Thus, I decided to try and ward off the tension and stress by keeping the kids busy. I followed a friend's example and brought play dough, pompoms, markers, paper, stickers, and other items the kids could use to craft.

I gathered the children up after dinner and took them to a table to work on their projects. There were three precious girls and a boy, ranging in ages from 4 to 10 years old. I unpacked the supplies, and they excitedly got to work doing whatever they wanted to do. As we worked, we talked and got to know each other. It was fun for the kids and for me, and the parents enjoyed having time to rest. We crafted all evening until it was time for the kids to get ready for bed and time for me to leave. We were sad the night was over.

I left the church and went out to my car where I sat for a while to type a text. Next thing I knew the four-year old girl was knocking on my window. She was outside getting ready to go take a shower in our shower trailer, and she saw me sitting there. I opened the window and she asked me why I was there and where I was going. I started to tell her that I was going home, but the word "home" hung in my throat when I looked in her beautiful green eyes and realized she had no home. Then I thought about her beautiful art projects and realized there was not even a family refrigerator where her parents could display her pictures. I reluctantly told her I was going to my house, and even that was painful for me to say. I went home with broken heart, a renewed appreciation for my home, and a memory I will never forget.

Like these families, we are not yet in our forever home; therefore, life is a struggle. Jesus said that while we are here, we will have hardships, but we can endure them because He is with us. We can have hope in knowing that when life ends here, we will begin a new life with Jesus in the eternal home He made especially for us.

> "There are many rooms in my Father's house. I wouldn't tell you this, unless it was true. I am going there to prepare a place for each of you" (John 14:2 CEV).

A Look Back

> "Forget the former things; do not dwell on the past. See, I am doing a new thing! Now it springs up; do you not perceive it? I am making a way in the wilderness and streams in the wasteland" (Isaiah 43:18-19 NIV).

I was surprised to receive videos on my phone recently from a guy who had been in the youth group of the church my husband had pastored in the mid-90's. These were no ordinary online videos; they were VHS video clips from the 1996 Christmas program at our church, specifically clips featuring my late husband leading the service.

It was so incredibly sweet to hear my husband's voice again and to see him standing in front of the church inviting people to accept Christ as their Savior. It was also wonderful to see my daughter, five years old at the time, joyfully playing a shepherd in the Christmas play. What I did not find so pleasant and wonderful was seeing myself at the age of 29.

I was a young mother and pastor's wife, learning each role as I went along. I was fighting a battle internally for control of my unexplained anger and doing my best to earn God's love by pleasing Him and serving others in His name. I had little self-esteem because my identity was wrapped up in who I was to others and my worth was determined by their opinion of me. I saw myself on the cusp of a devastating, life-and-death battle—my husband's battle against stage four, incurable brain cancer. In less than three years from the date of this video, I would lose my husband, my pastor, and our child's father.

As I thought about myself then, I couldn't help but take a hard look at myself now. I survived widowhood and single-motherhood. I chose to put myself in the care of Christian therapists who guided me through battles with my anger, depression, and grief, and discovered in the process that God loved me with a love I could not earn or lose. I found my value in Him as the beloved child of the Almighty God. Most amazing of all is that through this entire process toward healing, I developed a love for writing, which I later understood was God's gift to me as an avenue to share my story.

As my pastor said recently, brokenness is both the sickness and the cure. If I hadn't been broken, I would have never fought for wholeness. In the transformative process, God took my brokenness, turned it into strength and confidence, and gifted me with a way to tell others about it. I pray that through my writing, others will take courage from my redemption journey and find hope, strength, and value in the loving arms of God.

> "You came near when I called you, and you said, 'Do not fear.' You, Lord, took up my case; you redeemed my life" (Lamentations 3:57-58 NIV).

A Redemption Story

"Weeping may tarry for the night, but joy comes with the morning" (Psalm 30:5 ESV).

I received a text from my daughter that no parent wants to receive: "Mom, my car was just rear-ended." She then let me know she was fine and that there was no damage done to her car. A little while later, she sent me another text to tell me that on the way home, she suddenly got a painful headache and became sick to her stomach, so she decided to go to the hospital to get checked out. I met her there, and the doctors proceeded to run x-rays and scans to see if she had a serious injury. Tests showed she had only strained her neck, and the doctor told her to go home and take it easy for a while. A discharge nurse soon walked in and sat on the gurney beside my daughter to fill out the paperwork. I was surprised to see that I recognized the nurse as the daughter of friends who had grown up with my husband. My husband and her father had both died of cancer in their thirties.

I was captured by the moment. Sitting on the gurney together, the girls looked so much like their dads that I could easily picture their dads sitting there together as young men. My thoughts then turned to all that these two young women had been through in their lives. They both watched their dads suffer with cancer for years. Our two families simultaneously lived through years of cancer treatment, test results, and hospital stays while walking a long, fine, wavy line between hope and despair. The girls watched their dads slip into eternity taking years of their carefree childhood with them. They stood by and watched their moms grieve while working hard as single mothers to keep the family afloat. They both worried about losing their moms and what would happen to them if they did. They grew up, graduated from high school and college, and one of them married—all without their dads in attendance. Now here they are, two strong women, both trauma survivors, both working to help the sick and hurting.

God took our tragedies and used them for our good. It was not fair that our children grew up without their dads and we raised our girls without our husbands. However, God became our fathers and husbands and walked through our grief with us. He sustained us for years as we struggled to survive our severely broken hearts. Now here we are sitting in a hospital room—a nurse who is the daughter of a nurse; a social worker; and me, a church ministry assistant and devotional writer—all of us telling our stories and living out our callings to help people who are grieving and suffering. I know their fathers were there with us in our hearts. I could clearly picture them proudly watching us.

God never left us. He carried us through tragedy and is now standing with us on the other side. We are finally doing well, others are gaining strength from us, and God is rightfully receiving the glory. That is a true redemption story.

> "And we know that for those who love God all things work together for good, for those who are called according to his purpose" (Romans 8:28 ESV).

Prayer for a Fallen Police Officer's Family, Friends, City, and Colleagues[4]

> "So do not fear, for I am with you; do not be dismayed, for I am your God. I will strengthen you and help you; I will uphold you with my righteous right hand" (Isaiah 41:10 NIV).

Dear Father,
I pray for the family of this fallen police officer. I pray for his wife as she grieves for her husband and mourns her children's loss of their dad. Comfort her when she wishes she had more time for goodbyes and mourns all that was left unsaid. Please hold her when she angrily wrestles with regrets about her husband choosing a career that cost him his life and, as a consequence, she and her children have to live on without

him. If she wrestles with You, God, as to how You could have let this happen and whether you care, I pray that You will let her know that You are strong enough to take her anger and will love her through it. Please grant her peace beyond understanding and provide for her needs and the needs of her children in the coming days and years ahead.

I pray for the children. May they know their dad died a hero and that although he chose to protect our city, he did not choose to leave them as he did. I pray You will give peace to these children so that they do not live in fear of the world. I pray You will engrave the memories of their dad on their hearts so they always remember him as the dad they loved and who loved them dearly. Please send godly men to be role models for them who have the skills to mentor them as their own father would have done and in a way that honors You.

I pray for the officer's parents, extended family members, and close friends as they also mourn the loss of their loved one. I pray for wisdom as they struggle to walk the fine line between helping his family and intruding on their privacy. I pray that his wife will respond to them with love and understanding and will remain mindful of the fact that her children are all they have left of him. May his family draw closer and not allow this tragedy to tear them apart.

Finally, I pray for this police officer's colleagues and their families. Please provide the support they need to process this loss. Help the officers and their families as they let go of each other every day, knowing it may be the last time. I pray You will comfort those who witnessed the tragedy and may blame themselves for not preventing his death.

Please give our city leaders and residents wisdom in dealing with the aftermath of this tragedy. May our residents gather round this bereaved family and law enforcement community as a show of love, support, and encouragement. Please give us helpful words to say when we express our sympathy to the family.

Let this be a reminder to all of us to appreciate the risk our public servants and their families take every day to keep us safe. Let us hold our loved ones closer and keep them in our prayers daily, because You, O Lord, love them more than we do, and only You are able to be with them always.

Thank You, Lord, for being the gracious Father that You are to us. We love You. Amen.

End Notes

1   In the Garden. Written by C. Austin Miles (1913). Tune GARDEN by C. Austin Miles (1913). Public Domain. Retrieved from https://hymnary.org/text/i_come_to_the_garden_alone

2   Great Is Thy Faithfulness." Written by Thomas O. Chisholm (1923). Tune FAITHFULNESS composed by William M. Runyan (1923). Public Domain. Retrieved from https://hymnary.org/text/great_is_thy_faithfulness_o_god_my_fathe

3   *The Amazing Race*, "Get Your Sheep Together," Season 25, Episode 3. Directed by Bertram van Munster. Written by Elise Doganieri and Bertram van Munster. CBS Television Network, October 10, 2014

4   Written upon the shooting death of Maryville, Tennessee, Police Officer Kenneth Ray Moats. End of Watch: August 25, 2016.

Printed in the United States
By Bookmasters